INVESTING IN REAL ESTATE

FLIPPING HOUSES

THE STARTING GUIDE FOR REAL ESTATE BUSINESS
PLUS BUYING AND SELLING STRATEGIES FOR BEGINNERS

MIKE WEALTH

© Copyright 2020 by Mike Wealth - All rights reserved.

This Book is provided with the sole purpose of providing relevant information on a specific topic for which every reasonable effort has been made to ensure that it is both accurate and reasonable. Nevertheless, by purchasing this eBook you consent to the fact that the author, as well as the publisher, are in no way experts on the topics contained herein, regardless of any claims as such that may be made within. As such, any suggestions or recommendations that are made within are done so purely for entertainment value. It is recommended that you always consult a professional prior to undertaking any of the advice or techniques discussed within.

This is a legally binding declaration that is considered both valid and fair by both the Committee of Publishers Association and the American Bar Association and should be considered as legally binding within the United States.

The reproduction, transmission, and duplication of any of the content found herein, including any specific or extended information will be done as an illegal act regardless of the end form the information ultimately takes. This includes copied versions of the work both physical, digital and audio unless express consent of the Publisher is provided beforehand. Any additional rights reserved.

Furthermore, the information that can be found within the pages described forthwith shall be considered both accurate and truthful when it comes to the recounting of facts. As such, any use, correct or incorrect, of the provided information will render the Publisher free of responsibility as to the actions taken outside of their direct purview. Regardless, there are zero scenarios where the original author or the Publisher can be deemed liable in any fashion for any damages or hardships that may result from any of the information discussed herein.

Additionally, the information in the following pages is intended only for informational purposes and should thus be thought of as universal. As befitting its nature, it is presented without assurance regarding its prolonged validity or interim quality. Trademarks that are mentioned are done without written consent and can in no way be considered an endorsement from the trademark holder.

Table of Contents

Introduction 1

Chapter 1 Investing in Real Estate 3

Chapter 2 What Does It Mean to Flip Properties? 11

    Is There Anything You Need to Know About Flipping Houses? .. 13

    How Does Flipping Houses Work? 16

    Acquisition Method for Flipping 19

Chapter 3 False Myths about Flipping Houses 21

Chapter 4 The Right Mindset for Flipping Houses 26

Chapter 5 Have You Created a Business Plan? 31

    Have A Business Plan to Review Your Goals for the Year Ahead 32

    Your Business Plan Should Include 33

Chapter 6 Do You Need an Agent? 38

    Why Do You Need an Agent to Sell Your Home? 41

Chapter 7 How to Find Deals 43

    On Market Deals 46

Off Market Deals 49

Let's Talk About Lead Generation 50

Chapter 8 How to Find an Ideal Property 56

Tips to Consider before Purchasing an Investment Property 58

The Importance of Targeting Neighborhoods 61

Qualify the house 67

Next, Qualify the Seller 68

The House Analysis 68

Make an Offer 74

Chapter 9 Financial Analyses of a Potential Deal 76

Chapter 10 Negotiation Tips when Buying a House 84

The 100-10-1 Rule 91

Mistakes Not to Do while Making Offers 94

Chapter 11 Financing 99

Chapter 12 How to Choose the Right Loan for You 104

Flipping When You Have no Money 106

Chapter 13 Leverage or Not? 108

Chapter 14 Loans vs. Other People's Money 112

Chapter 15 Home Renovation 122

The 4 Kinds of Home Renovations 129

Chapter 16 Renovation Goals 134

Chapter 17 Tips to Increase Home Value 141

Chapter 18 Tips for a Successful Closing 148

Chapter 19 Price Home Correctly 155

    Home Staging 156

    The Price is Right 160

    How Fast Should a Flip Be Completed? 162

    Of Appraisals and Selling Price 163

Chapter 20 Selling Your Home – Negotiation Tips 165

Chapter 21 Mistakes Not to Make when Flipping Houses 172

Chapter 22 Why Others Fail in Real Estate 178

Chapter 23 How to Face Future Risks 186

Conclusion 195

Introduction

Many years ago, the word "flipping" wasn't a household term, and only a few people related the word to properties and profit-making. People never wanted to sell their properties, even in the worst circumstances. They only sold if it was their last resort until the economic recession in the United States made a lot sell their homes to survive. Recently, not only house builders, contractors, electricians, and carpenters make money from houses, but some young entrepreneurs also make money from real estate even without having any knowledge of the profession. These people are called house flippers. Flipping is a lucrative business with a mouthwatering salary; however, it is also risky and can be stressful if things didn't go as planned.

There is a cordial relationship between flipping and real estate, but flipping is used to describe short term real estate transactions. The term flipping is a process that deals with the purchase of an asset and selling it out. In flipping, the investors acquire assets, add improvement of some kind, control them, and sell within a short period for profit. Flipping applies to stocks, shares, and real estate. In other cases, it can also be used for cars, sports tickets, and concert tickets. The primary aim of any form of flipping is to make a profit. Flipping can be done in politics, IPOs, technical trading, professional fund, management, car, and real estate. IPOs mean Initial Public Offering. IPO happens when the shares of a company are made accessible for the public to own/purchase. Most companies sell their property cheaply during this period, which ensures that the property is quickly purchased. The people that buy IPO shares and sell them out to make a profit are referred to as IPO flippers. For real estate, flipping has an offensive meaning. It is believed that it is used to describe an investor that buys a house at miserable amounts or the lowest possible price to renovate to boost its value. It is also related to manipulation in the market, which may be associated with socially destructive and unethical activities, fraud, and dulling people of their properties to make huge profits. Flipping is also applicable in macro funds that require the use of broad market trends. The managers of macro funds may decide on flipping sectors to sense potential losses and divert the gains to profitable sectors.

However, in recent times, most people have viewed real estate flipping as a respectable and regular business. Car flipping has also made ground, and it refers to the purchase of a car at a lower price and selling it at a higher price. The people who are involved in this act are referred to as car flippers, and they are trained at bargaining prices for flipping both buying and selling of the properties. However, this book is limited to the house flipping. Fortunately, however, learning the ins and outs of real estate can be a whole lot less complicated, especially if you've got a guide like this one.

Chapter 1
Investing in Real Estate

Starting a real estate business is a daunting task. It may not be that easy looking at those who have made it in the area and concluding it's a walk in the park. It takes a lot of hard work, good decision making, patience, tolerance, and learning. If you are ready to pick lines from the gurus in the area, you will find running a real estate an easy task. However, you may need to be more determined to get your business up by investing everything. For most of the people in the industry, they have experienced hardships in the first year of starting the business, and those who are brave make it higher.

Getting into the real estate business does not need you to expect more than you can offer. You need to concentrate on building it fast than thinking about the profits and how you will handle it. Rather start by learning ways on how to make it better and grow. You need not get distracted on the way as that may lead to your failure early in the business. Make sacrifices and ensure you have gained what it takes to be the best in the industry. It is not easy at first, but once you get used to it, you will grow to love it.

The real estate business is an interesting industry as you get to meet different people, locations, buildings, and so on. You first need to love it to do it. If you keep the mentality that you can do it without loving it, this is not for you. It's also not for the fainted hearted as it requires a lot of work and sacrifices to pick up.

What is the real estate business all about?

Before going into the industry, you need to be well versed in what you are dealing with. You should understand all the aspects of real estate and how it works.

Real estate is considered as a property that includes land, buildings, natural resources, crops, roads, and other immovable things. It can also be the professional activities of selling, renting, and buying land and generally houses. It also deals with human activity that is involved in making improvements to the land. On the other hand, real property deals with the rights that a property has. For instance, the interests that come from human activities.

Why choose the real estate business?

The real estate business is a fast-growing investment strategy that takes more than hard work. You need to be dedicated and sacrifices to make sure your needs are met. However, they may be affected by market changes or conflict, and you need to know what type of real estate business you need to venture into. It is so interesting working on something you love and feel safe handling. It is always hard at first but can turn out to be the best over time.

Deciding to embark on the real estate business takes a lot of courage and commitment. However hard it may be at the beginning, there is always a greater reward in the future. Here are the reasons as to why you have to consider real estate business:

- **It is so easy to get in:** Unlike other professionals who take a longer to get employment or while studying, the real estate industry does not require a lot of skills to become one. You can be a real estate agent with a limited number of skills or knowledge and learn more on the way. Once you get in, you will easily fit in. In most firms, there are several part-time workers or students too. It's easier to learn and adapt. The knowledge you seek is always within your reach. For example, you can acquire it from the realtors or your mentors.

- **There is an easier profit-making:** Starting on your business may not be that simple. However, once you have mastered how to grow your business and know how to get more clients to buy the real estate you are selling, you will automatically feel a boost in your bank. It is a lucrative industry and working hard for profits is essential. Once you work hard, you are sure to get something in return at all times.
- **You will more likely work hard:** As much as it is easy to work hard for your business, you may need to have a form of appreciation for what you do. You should feel and experience the results of your hard work in a unique way. The more the hard work, dedication, and determination, the easier it is to receive positive results.
- **It is interesting:** You will not have that life of a professional who always sits in an office from Monday to Monday, getting bored and feeling like quitting. Several trends change, markets, and the environment. You will most likely be at the field or place of construction to see if it's taking the right direction. You may even interact with people who see life from a different

perspective and sharing experiences will be even more worthwhile.

What you should expect in the real estate business?

Most people make a mistake of expecting everything to turn out easy as they may have thought. This is not the case with real estate businesses. They are faced with a lot of competition, and you need to keep your business up to be the best. You need to invest in your business and strive to make it unique as much as possible to remain relevant. If you are willing to learn and sacrifice, you will surely get the deserving results.

Here is what you need to keep in mind when starting your business:

- **Not an easy task:** Starting the real estate business may not be that rosy at first, as it will take a toll on your time and sleep, thinking about the best ways to grow and improve your businesses. You may need to research a lot on the market, the location of the property as well as the gents you will use to get clients, and so on. To ensure everything is going on smoothly, it will take a lot of hard work, determination, and sacrifice. Success and profits will not come on easily. It takes time and perseverance. You should not be faint-hearted if you need to experience success. Always keep in mind the idea that you have crossed the battle line, and you have to do everything it takes to emerge the winner.
- **Be creative:** For any real estate business, you should expect to

CHAPTER 1: Investing in Real Estate

be more open to ideas. Learning new things and how well to solve the challenges in the real world will help you grow your business. As much as you have the knowledge and expertise in your profession, it will take more than to come up with the right decision to help you grow. You do not have to rely on your family and friends to help you solve your work issues. Being your boss comes with many responsibilities that need you to be reliable and go beyond your comfort zone to see you grow into a successful real estate agent. You will learn how to handle your issues peacefully within yourself and use the most innovative and creative ideas to help your business improve and make the decisions right for it.

- **You will need help:** When starting your business, you are probably afraid of getting new experiences. At the same time, you may find yourself excited about seeing your business grow. As you may be new in the industry, you may need somewhere to lay your shoulder on. You may have to ask for help with running your business. Most real estate agents use brokers (salespeople who have expertise and experience in negotiating deals). They are a great resource for the growth of your business. They will prepare you for what you will meet on the way to your success and how you need to finalize deals or decide on the property value as long as they have been on the market. They work on a commission, and they navigate the market easily to get you potential customers. Where you are not well versed, you should feel free to ask those who have experience in the industry. Who knows, you may learn a thing or two on how to improve your business. Before gaining more knowledge and experience, you will pass through challenges that will require you to make the right decision for your team or business. Listening to other people's experiences would help you make it right.

- **Make room for disappointments:** Like any other business out there, you need to make room for failures. It may not be that easy to be relevant in the industry within a day. It takes a lot of time and effort to become somebody. You may feel like giving up at some point in the journey, but reminding yourself why you chose to start it in the first place may help you remain firm. At some point, you will be disappointed by your team or the tenants you sold or rented a house to. In most situations, the tenants are always hard to handle and want to control you, but getting good ones takes a miracle. Always be prepared for disappointments will save you from heartbreak all the time as you had already prepared your mind of failures once something negative comes about. By easily accepting mistakes and learning from them will greatly help. You can learn to take things easy next time. It's simple and effective once you plan for its possibility. Choosing to ignore and handling issues amicably should keep you going. You can strive to make yourself better.
- **Profits:** Real estate businesses are very popular with successful profits. Once you have mastered the art of convincing your

potential clients into buyers, you may have to sit and wait for your bank alert. It takes a lot of time and patience, but once you have a perfect property most people are yearning for, you will easily sell them. You need to research the kind of location that mostly fits a particular type of real estate business and strive to get properties of the best quality. Not overpricing will get you more clients. As small the profits may be at first, you can invest them in a more meaningful way to help secure your future and save you during tax payment. It is a lucrative business, and it reaps benefits.

- **You need to grow your business:** Once you start a business, you need to look for ways to make it grow. Consider using your knowledge, expertise, and influence to grow the leads and networks. You need to build relationships with people. The more people know you, the more there will be potential buyers. It may not be an easy task, but you need to market yourself. Let people know what you are selling or what you are into. Putting yourself out there will greatly help you make the right networks. You can simply connect with your family and friends, attend community gatherings, and use online platforms for marketing you as a brand. However, it may not be simple as you need to sacrifice a lot to get what you are looking for.

Chapter 2
What Does It Mean to Flip Properties?

Houses get old, so the owner sells them to a fixer-up who then fixes, renovates and then sells them. This is what is known as house flipping or flipping houses. Want to know what flipping houses are? Flipping houses is when an investor of a real estate buys houses and sell it with

CHAPTER 2: What Does It Mean to Flip Properties?

the aim of making profit, houses which are considered to be flipped should be sold out quickly. Timing the purchase period and the sales period ranges from 2-6 months and most times almost up to a year.

You might have seen TV shows, read local newspapers and blogs on real estate home flipping. I am sure you find it very entertaining but definitely, these shows, and local newspapers are lacking in full practical information that you would need to get started in this industry. It might look frustrating but basically, you should understand how the business works.

It looks easy, right? Yes, but also risky, but with the guides and tactics provided in this book, you will get to see that if you're good enough at buying houses that won't cost you much fixing, your aim of making a profit would be quickly achieved.

In the business of real estate flipping, you need to know how to find houses, analyze them and buy them. Finding a house, analyzing it and buying it without proper guidance can be very costly to yourself and others. Now the process of fixing the home will add value to the home. An investor should know that when buying a property, the property should have a potential increase in value with updates, with a target of selling out the property for higher prices than what they purchased it for.

Now, having known what house flipping is, we are focusing on what the definition is. House flipping can be done in the right way and also in the wrong way. How? With a smart renovation, you can make much more money than what you paid for. You should have heard the worst stories of flipping houses, where it looks like a good deal having a house with a bad foundation and a leaking roof. When you have decided on flipping a house, you wouldn't want to lose money by making a wise investment and reap. I'm sure you won't mind if I am giving out the secret behind flipping houses with an easy step. Before flipping houses, you should consider having an agent in that field, they might have the same ideas in common but get the right agent.

Now back to the steps behind flipping houses; firstly, get a real estate agent (Expert) that can guide you through knowing the market, having done this, get an outline of your budget upfront, network with contractors, analyze the market, know your market, invest in reasonable renovations and see to making a profit. Also, always keep your updates on track and don't forget that big renovations like the kitchen can break your flip budget. A detailed real estate agent can provide you the guidance needed to make a smart investment.

Is There Anything You Need to Know About Flipping Houses?

Finding a mentor, making research, learn to negotiate, there's no fixed price no matter how beautiful or how conducive the house is, you should learn to beat down the price when buying a house, learn your market and lastly, understand your finances. Let's look into how flipping can be illegal, more reasons why you should get an expert in the field. Flipping can be illegal if the property is resold for an inflated value.

CHAPTER 2: What Does It Mean to Flip Properties?

Flipping houses is another way of making money in the real estate business as an act of buying a house, fixing things and selling it for more than you originally purchased it for. Flipping simply means buying a house and selling it out quickly for a profit. **Is house flipping for you?** Yes! As long as you have a budget and an expert to guide you, then you are good to go. The main reason people sell their house at their comfort is that they are not willing to renovate it due to low or non-existent capital. Beyond that, most people would prefer a move-in ready home. Looking into a detailed explanation about flipping houses, we see that it has now become a highly popular real estate investment type. This is because it has a high potential of giving you a very good profit. When you buy a home, it's always necessary to fix what is needed to be repaired, the kitchen and bathroom in one word, it's as though you're adding value to it for a good profit selling.

Would you rather rent a house or flip? Let see the difference between flipping a house and renting a house. Basically, flipping a house requires active participation while renting a house earns you passive income monthly, isn't this great? Flipping a house and renting a house makes you earn money. Tax rules for flipped houses are treated as an income with tax rates between 20% and 47%, no capital gains with a lower tax rate of 0% to 20%. How can flipping be profitable to real estate investors, you may not think you're in business because you take flipping houses as a side project to make extra money, as a real estate investor either you're buying properties under LLC or with your name,

INVESTING IN REAL ESTATE: Flipping Houses

as you operate as a business with a real estate that's investing a business plan, that's the more you're aiming to make a profit.

For how long should you hold a house? When you hold a property for almost a year and selling it out for a profit this is referred to as short term capital gain, and when you hold a property for 13-15 months, now, your profit is no longer a short term gain, it's now a long term capital gain, Why? Because you owned the investment for more than a year.

You would have asked yourself if flipping houses brings you extra passive income apart from the fixing and damages. Yes, it does. However, you need to ensure you buy a good property and get experts to remodel and sell them. Like I earlier noted, you would make tons of money flipping houses when you find cheap houses, buy them, fix them up and resell the houses for a huge profit.

Does flipping houses have requirements? Continue reading and know that you shouldn't get a house flipping with lousy credit and also if you don't have great credit, you need to start building a good credit score. Have a notable plan of making your great credit score increase.

When buying a house without sizeable down payment, make use of your credits cards to pay for the house renovation. For you to be a successful flipper you need plenty cash to start up. Most times, traditional lenders require a down payment of 30% and they would give you a good rate, but when you provide cash for your down payment, you won't have to pay for private mortgage insurance.

When using a loan to flip, it requires high interest rate, that's why most

CHAPTER 2: What Does It Mean to Flip Properties?

investors prefer taking out an interest-only loan. At the average, the interests of this type of loan is 10% to 14%. What do you suggest? Paying in cash, right? Yes. Paying in cash for less interest.

How Does Flipping Houses Work?

Have you flip a house before? Here is how you go about it, fixing and flipping especially a flat in the real estate market. There are a lot of decisions to make from starting:

1. Where should you buy it?

Buying a house in an up-and-coming neighborhood, you're already banking on the increase in value but when you make decisions buying in a new development, you will want it to be attractive to higher-end buyers who are willing to get a luxury features and space.

If it ends really well, then you would make a very good profit. But if it turns out to be otherwise, budget with faults, issues with timing in that up and coming neighborhood could stick you with a house you can't get rid of.

2. Do you know what you want to buy?

Once you know where to buy, your next step should be the type of property you are purchasing. You might want to go for a fixer-upper that means you want to commit to improving the house which will take much of your time and money. Conversely, you can choose to purchase a foreclosed property from a bank, this would help you get a good bargain on the underpriced house.

But note that if the previous owner can't afford to pay for the mortgage, they probably can't lay for the upkeep, either, so you might have real issues with the house itself. Do not be surprised if you find a leaky roof in the house you just bought.

I bring you good news for you to begin real estate investing. You don't necessarily need to have a capital to buy property with cash. Rather, you can get someone who helps borrowers with buyers that have heavy cash. So, it's better to make your mistakes with a smaller loan.

3. Can you invest in small?

You can invest small and smart. Don't go for the burst pipes and holes in the ceiling. You might likely turn a profit with houses that do not need fixing issues with so much. Rather, you might need to take care of some minor issues, and then sell the house for a higher price. With this process, it would be easier for you to convince and entice the buyer when less risk occurs, especially if it's your very first time into real estate investing.

4. Do you know that you need to know how much it would cost you to renovate?

I mean, you should know how much the renovated property is worth and how much it will cost to flip. Doing your research and understanding the basics, you might get a profitable house flipping and most

CHAPTER 2: What Does It Mean to Flip Properties?

importantly, consider the cost of financing.

Do your research before you make the final decision on what to invest in. It always helps.

5. Have you gotten the right neighborhood?

Not all neighborhoods are bad. Most importantly, know the depth knowledge of the market you want to invest in. Let's do a sample research for getting the right neighborhood.

6. How many homes are you selling for?

Firstly, know the average price and the types of the home being sold. If your agent is a real estate agent, he should know the amount of home sold in the past year and recent sales, searching through MLS, he can get you a report quickly for you to do online research.

7. Have you calculated the months of supply with your agent?

If you want to know how quickly homes are selling, you should calculate the "months of supply" what does "months of supply" means, it means the number of months it would take to sell all the homes that are currently on the market which helps to realize it you're in a buyer's or seller's market.

Your questions should be how to know if you're in a buyer's or seller's using the months of supply: Buyer's market, the months of supply is over six months while the Seller's market, the month is lower than six months.

8. Have you made your research on market trends that will affect home prices?

Once you have gotten a firm pricing in your market, you need to figure out where the prices are going to be in the next couple of years. Read blogs, national press and newspapers, these would help you find market trends, to identifying deals worth pursuing, you would know the market and a few surrounding neighborhoods.

9. Have you advertised to find projects?

Advertise to find deals and projects for you to make money.

10. Have you gotten the right house?

Go in search of vacant homes, try as much as possible to get in touch with the owners, the owner might be ready to move for some reasons, maybe he/she needs money. The success of accomplishing this is reaching out to the direct homeowner.

Reach out to people who are broke and poor that are willing to sell. Network with them. Do you know why it works? It works because brokers and real estate experts may not have the time or probably may not have the connection to flip a home, but by doing this, you've succeeded.

Acquisition Method for Flipping

Let's break down the buying of a home and how it works. This will help

CHAPTER 2: What Does It Mean to Flip Properties?

you determine the method for acquiring the properties of the home you're buying. From working with real estate agent and buying house listed on MLS.

- **Do you know what MLS is?** It means (Multiple Listing Service) i.e., to buy at auction (buying online, bank owned) to market for and working with private sellers.
- **Farm Area.** The size of the farm area depending on your experience for buying strategies may increase the size of your farm with time. When starting out, focus on a small location and get used to the area by knowing your neighborhood and the street, with the expectation of knowing what to do to those houses that can bring up value.
- **The type of house you should focus on buying.** You should focus on 2-3-bedroom flats with a standard "entry-level" price range. Also, focus on homes that need updating and works, examples like kitchen and bathroom (basic repair). Do not go for houses that have borehole issues, pipes and other things that would cost you to spend much money and time on.
- **The deal analysis.** To avoid dying in the water business understand how to analyze and evaluate the house. Deal analysis is the business that holds the cement together Therefore, you shouldn't run your business without understanding this critical skill!

Chapter 3
False Myths about Flipping Houses

One of the false myths people believe generally is that you need money to make money, and am like really? But I would confuse you with this and make you see that house owners don't get the right information when they want to sell their home.

One of the most common misconceptions about this **business is that real estate is reserved for the wealthy**. This is why most people think they need to first save a great deal of income to purchase a property. Of

CHAPTER 3: False Myths about Flipping Houses

course, we know that money makes things easier but it's possible to get a property with no money of your own when you follow the right mindset. At the end of this chapter, we would make you see that following the right mindset of flipping houses can help you purchase one.

A bad credit won't be able to get you funding; getting a loan through the bank is a proper way, but when you don't have a good credit, loans won't be possible. You would also need a private sector which can be your family member, your colleague or friend, one of these people should have an expendable income to invest. But if getting those people might be difficult to get and flipping seems like failing, you could try get loan from hard money lenders work. Banks are hard money lenders. But you will be charged a huge percentage on top of your interest.

Have you tried to work with someone as a partner? When you have no money or credit, the partner would fund the money but you will do most of the work, take a look at this, it's just that the person is helping you raise the funds but you're the one in need of the business except otherwise if the person is interested too.

How can real estate be risky? **Most times, investing in property can be risky.** Sometimes, the market would depreciate, and problem occurs. This definitely would cause huge losses for any real estate investor.

There is a way this myth can be handled. Have you considered wholesaling? As a first-time real estate investor, you can try this out.

INVESTING IN REAL ESTATE: Flipping Houses

For your first project, a standard fix and flip business can be in two ways, either make-up or breakup. This is the safer road for first time real estate investors. If wholesaling is done properly, you do not have to spend or borrow money. Rather than borrowing or spending, you should find a property or put it under contract, get a buyer and sit back to enjoy your wholesaler's fee in return.

Anything you take part with, make sure you do your research well. You have to be a contractor before flipping houses. In most cases, most people will hire a team for their rehab which is good and quick but would cost more money but basically less stress.

How would you go about start selling right away; you might have heard this, or you should know that **the longer the property is on hold to sell, the more you lose money**. Insurance, tax and maintenance will cost you monthly, in other for you not to run into vandalism, don't hold the house for a long time. The fact is that you should sell as quickly as possible, you don't have to.

You would need this: instead of wholesaling, fix and flip, you can try to buy and hold, it helps too, here is how you go about it. Firstly, rent out the property to tenants for a monthly income, pending the time you would see a buyer. Secondly, you can hold the home till it appreciates and then put it up for a sale, for a great and better value.

The best time to sell is the early summertime. That is what most people believe. I mean, late December and early January. But how did I go about this? Well, I believe that most people will take advantage of the time they have by spending the festive period in their new homes and sometimes it can be a normal relocation. I would consider you selling it out around New Year. Wow, how true can this be.

You can get rich quick; oh, like seriously? Don't be deceived, there's no real way to get money quick. Investing requires hardworking, investing sometimes might be looking sluggish but the best thing is to keep at what you do, and it takes time to be successful, it's one step at a time.

You should know that, you would not just get all your riches from one flip, why don't you just increase your income, take your time and also minimize your skills and not cutting corners. I hope I am clear with that, don't recalibrate your mindset, it's one step at a time.

You should find a perfect house for flipping. Recognize values, example, a strong foundation and a good neighborhood. Try and find the faults of a house before buying it to avoid much cost on renovations. A lot of attributes about faulty homes can't be seen in one property, it's nearly impossible. Doing the best, you can, you should also know that, no house is perfect. So, I would tell you that, you should stop wasting time finding the right and perfect house to flip.

Pick a house, do your calculation and see if it worth buying. Did I just say that, it is quick and easy better than a normal job, okay, let's move forward? Easy and quick maybe achievable but also may be impossible.

INVESTING IN REAL ESTATE: Flipping Houses

Are you afraid of asking? If you're not sure how long flipping should take but set a time frame for completing works based on the plan and the quality trade people.

You can make some good money; Investors encounter issues that can lead to an argument and also provides some drama, not how far? But how well it is, having to get the job done, they make solid returns.

It is easy to assume that every flip should be or is going to be successful. Real estate is a great investment vehicle and more likely to appreciate than depreciate. So, you can actually see reasons why I stated that flipping is risky, it's either you win or lose, like I would always say to myself, Be Consistent, Consistency is key. A good plan will be the basis of achieving projects on time. Have a plan and process it.

More money, more profit. An important step to figure out how to achieve your goals is knowing your 'Why'. If you don't mind, why not create a business you love, and get a life you enjoy living. Having known your 'why', you will find or have the courage to take risks in business and life generally.

Chapter 4

The Right Mindset for Flipping Houses

The type of mindset you need to be successful when it comes to flipping houses:

Do you have an entrepreneurial spirit?

Can you work diligently or efficiently?

Do you have a passion for flipping houses?

Do you have courage?

And lastly, can you take risks?

Once you can answer these questions yourself, you can proceed and if you can't, you might get burnt-out quickly.

Have you learned what it takes to become a successful house flipper? Now, you know that house flipping is not easy the way it is, and it takes a person with a determined mindset to be successful at it. Flipping

INVESTING IN REAL ESTATE: Flipping Houses

houses requires a different skills and experience including real estate sales, real estate laws, project management and accounting, interior designs, constructions.

Do you need a formal education? No. But an experience will help you build a strong foundation. Experiences in this field are very helpful, just identify your strength and weakness and build house flipping team that can help you scale your business.

Along the line, your team will act as your teachers. So, why do you need to call your attorney? If you need to ask a question about the construction process, the method, materials or any question pertaining to flipping houses, you can call him/her. First, flipping can be a bit disturbing because you will have a lot of questions, issues and mostly

CHAPTER 4: The Right Mindset for Flipping Houses

problems and your team will help out along the way.

Following the right mindset about flipping house is a way to generate extra income while you have a full-time working job. It sounds great. Without holding anything back, as an entrepreneur, mindset is everything.

To avoid losing a lot of money, your mindset is important, you don't underestimate your mindset to succeed in flipping houses. Take this, you should love everything you do in life, flipping houses can be hard and stressful, it takes time and energy, only the strong survives. You must run it like one at all times, it's boring but must be done, that's why you need to love what you do.

The most pertaining to do so as to get the right mindset is that, you must be willing to roll up when deal goes awful, be prepared to check on your projects every day and personally manage every project. For a consistent success in real estate, you mustn't blame others when a deal goes wrong or doesn't work out, the more you put blame on them, the more issue you have, not to mention, it makes you look unprofessional.

You always want to take 100% responsibility for your actions, it seems difficult to some and to be honest, it can be quite herculean to do so.

Also, people who blame markets and other investors or client will always continue to have issues. Opening yourself to more opportunities is when you take responsibility of your actions.

Like I said earlier, mentioning frustration, deals were slow for me, almost crawling, I thought about what I could do to get deals, but I couldn't believe how things went for me on my business.

To encompass a ceaseless desire, a good entrepreneur will learn and take risk, making use of their past experience to shape their success path.

The greatest mistake you should avoid is not taking advantage, stories and the advice of other entrepreneurs, in business as a learner you shouldn't try to be a hero, learn from other folks, learn from their success and mistakes. Real estate agent makes mistakes and still share their experiences in other to save other people from falling into the same trap. I have had a lot of mistakes and I am still learning, that's why I am telling you now to learn from people who you wouldn't mind trading with.

Commitment: For you to be successful in this business you have to be committed and love the grind. Having to strive your own venture is hard as a real estate entrepreneur. In every business, strive to work hard to make a profitable money.

Stay focus, love the process of your business, be committed through the good and bad time. To lead your business to success, always learn, learning is the mindset that you must comprehend.

In and out of any business, all you need to focus on is continual learning, and developing a strong business mindset. For the newbies, set aside 2 hours per day or more to actively expand your knowledge of the real estate business. Do you know that your desire to learn is a rewarding asset? So, in any successful business, learning is necessary.

CHAPTER 4: The Right Mindset for Flipping Houses

Chapter 5
Have You Created a Business Plan?

If you don't put the right stuff at the right time, you might not get the result you desire. You may have a plan for your investment, and your business plan should include the marketing plan, mission statement and more.

CHAPTER 5: Have You Created a Business Plan?

Have A Business Plan to Review Your Goals for the Year Ahead

A successful house flipper begins with a solid business plan, in this process, you would find the right professionals, you would obtain financing and the final steps is to market and sell your flip for profit. A financing partner would be included in your business plan and needed for you to start flipping a house.

You need a business plan with definable goals when you're learning how to buy and flip houses, this business would help to figure out projects that would make you achieve your goals for a complete work, this would encourage lenders to take you seriously and put your profit expectations.

It takes patience and time to create real estate goals. Identifying areas of growth and improvement can help investors target their marketing plan and investment, I would say that you should review your business plan ask questions from your mentor, ask people, ask business partners in the same field with you.

A business plan conforms to influence real estate goal settings. These goals mentioned above can have a lasting influence on the path your career takes.

What your specific goals should look like? Now that you want to make profit and you want to improve, I believe your goal should be more than "I want to" and should be "I want to improve and increase my profit this year so as to enable me increase next year marketing budget". You should start by evaluating, creating a physical checklist yourself and strike out each stage of goal as you achieve it. I said that to say this, go extra mile to give yourself an advantage. By the time you're drafting out each goal ask yourself questions like:

Why is my goal important?

What do you need to achieve the goal?

Who will be involved to accomplish this goal successfully?

When you're done answering these questions, there's nothing delaying you, just get out there and start making moves.

Your Business Plan Should Include

House flipping business is aimed at, to make a profit, it is very essential to know what to include in your business plan that is why you should you need to do your research well. Investors and lenders go through your business plan, that's why you need to make it easy to understand and include information.

1. Summary Goal. Your summary should also include, specific purposes; how to achieve them depends on the types of properties like single household home, duplex and so on. The geographical area should be around where you purchase and flip the property, while the contractors will do their work and your project timeline shouldn't be

CHAPTER 5: Have You Created a Business Plan?

more than 90 days.

2. Include your market analysis. Get the price trends in your area and target the upcoming development in your area.

3. Now you need to decide if you are sure of **cash savings** or **financial sources**. However, financing may enable you to buy and renovate more properties at once. Let's say, you have $80,000 to flip a house, now, you make use of the savings to purchase and renovate a single home and then flips it for $120,000, which means you just made $20,000 without having to incur any borrowing costs. You can actually see that this is a good deal, right? This means when you have your own personal savings you can actually gain more profits without a debt.

4. Your trade sales and plan. Trade sales and plan covers how to sell or market your rehabbed property, even when you're hiring an agent or to sell on your own. In this your notable plan, include how you market the property and the steps you would take to sell the property.

5. Personal Bios. Your personal biographies should be included in your business plan for house flipping to provide insight, it should also consist of an adequate paragraph, highlight of your qualification and education.

6. Hiring the right flipping professionals: solicitor, contractors, accountant, real estate agents, by getting these sets of people, you would need to do online research and asses well by checking the reviews. To ensure that your business is following the legal guidelines, all you need is a professional that flip houses. Basically, professionals can be hired per project.

Here are some house flipping pros you should hire as I noted earlier:

- **Attorney:** select an attorney that specialized in real estate, this would make him or her help your business in observation with local regulation.
- **Contractor:** ensure that your general contractor is licensed in the same area where you work, so that he can attend to your rehabs, without a general contractor you have to attend to the job site yourself.
- **Handyperson:** he doesn't need to be authorized, they are hired for painting, patching holes in the home.
- **Landscaper:** for your home not to lack curb appeal, they should be hired on, as-needed basis.
- **Real estate agent:** before flipping in a house, they would give you more valid data, because they are learned and gives you accurate information.
- **Architect:** they should be used for structural integrity for the house not to become more compromised. They are required for larger projects like, changing the house layout or structures and also adding on rooms. To avoid spending unnecessary money that would cost you thousands of dollars, they should be hired.
- **Assistant:** now that you would have met with the right professionals, hiring an assistant to help you every day with

CHAPTER 5: Have You Created a Business Plan?

business activities isn't a bad idea. Now that we have seen what you need before starting as a newbie, let's see some important rules before hiring a professional.

An expert should be referred to you from someone you know and has success with this person, because referrals are always the best, mostly the trusted source. But the fact that he was referred to you doesn't mean it's a guarantee, a long-time person can offer you a referral, family, and friends can offer you referrals, but the most beneficial ones come from other investors. But always ensure that the professionals know how to do the job you're hiring him for, it actually saves you money.

If a job is done poorly in the first time, that means you would have to pay for the same job twice, this is the main reason why you have to inform your experts what you're hiring him for, it saves you time and money.

7. Registration. Now you would decide on how your business should be set up. Have you heard about EID? When the registration commences you will have to register with the IRS to get an employee identification number (EID) which recognizes it as a business entity. Check within your state for other business permission you may need.

Take note that, whether you're running your flipping business at the comfort of your own home or in the office, those steps mention earlier need to be followed.

8. Business bank account. I'm sure by now you would have gotten your

EID number, you can make use of this EID number to open a business bank account. It prevents the commingling of your business and personal money. When your accountant does your taxes, it helps you eradicate auditing from the IRS.

9. Request for a credit card. Also, you should have a business bank account by now, along the line, we suggest that you should apply for a business credit card so as to help you purchase building materials, office furniture, and office equipment.

You may not have an idea about how the investment group loan looks like. After joining an investment group and you have a little experience in real estate, they may be willing to put up some cash for your deals, most likely.

10. Buy, Rehab and sell properties. By now you're ready to buy, fix in and sell for a profit. Normally it takes 10 to 25 days to close on a property using cash and may also take 40 to about 130 days to rehab the property depending on the condition.

Social media most times will be needed in cases like this, how? Once the rehab is complete enough to take photos you should start marketing the property.

Put in mind that, property may be sold out in a few days or months depending on the local market and pricing.

Chapter 6
Do You Need an Agent?

You need an expert; you need real estate professionals that would help you light up your business deal. The flexibility of schedule is what real estate expert does, they help with one of the largest bargains of their lives.

As agents, these people are able to provide more benefits since they are real estate experts. The percentage of agents who failed to succeed in their business is rarely discussed. Basically, nearly 7- 10 newbies agents can be expected to fail which is just an eye-opener. Getting as an expert who was referred are the best, now you need to know if the expert is hardworking.

1. A hardworking expert

Being an entrepreneur puts up with a lot of hard work. So, most reasons why they fall is because they didn't work hard enough, they should work long hours, they should workday and night available on social media via phone.

Advice: learning is what agents should do every day to become more successful. It's important for you to have enough money to save so as to enable you to buy life requirements.

Real estate business is not for everyone, you shouldn't get involved in the business for the wrong reason. Let me tell you a real estate myths and actually the furthest from the truth, most people think real estate agent make huge money, but the main reason why some people attempt to sell is because they think real estate agent make boatloads of money.

Real estate agents know how important it is to spend money to build their business but using real estate marketing strategies to sell home costs more money. Most times why you would need an agent is because it saves you more time and most of these agents has access to many properties, they would help you get information and negotiate with it. Good agents have detailed information to help you make decision, they

CHAPTER 6: Do You Need an Agent

would handle a lot of work on your behalf.

Most agents have access to an online platform where they buy homes that are recorded for sale, not just everybody can list properties on sale, the only people that can do that are licensed realtors and can also collect a commission for supplying the buyer for a transaction.

Aside from being a seller or buyer as an agent, they also work in a property management whereby they combine skills to earn.

2. Real estate agent would help you network

I would suggest that, knowing more people in the local real estate is better, and also have it in mind that having a real estate agent would help you saves time.

License real estate can supplement their house flipping income with their real estate commission. Having a real estate agent is just a strong advantage for you. Real estate agents would always get your back if you're buying or selling a house. They are bound to put their buyers or sellers first.

One of the reason why you would need an agent is because they know what to look for, including areas, the sizes and why you should or should not buy a particular house, getting a real estate agent who is good and is specialized in that field will be alert for some issues which might not have crossed your mind such as a leaking roof, insect problems and so on like that. Agents recognize these problems and know how to touch them. Now, we can actually see that your agent's knowledge has saved you thousands. If you're a seller, you know how much you want for your home, but the price you arrived at, is it reasonable? But if you can identify this sale that you're in the right range or not, that means you know because agents do a market analysis.

If you don't know how to start that means you have a lot of time-consuming research to do on your own.

3. Agents and their skills

Agents are good when it comes to negotiating because they get the best possible deal on the property you're buying. They are trained to negotiate well from experiences because they know what really works and what does not.

Why Do You Need an Agent to Sell Your Home?

Let's say you have a buyer, but an agent will help you net more on your bottom line, in the seller's market, anyone can entice offers by putting a home for sale, in this type of situation get yourself prepared to handle multiple offers and extracting money from buyers. You may be losing exposure of 75% of the buying population if you don't hire an agent.

Real estate agents bring added value: it brings value to the transaction, the experienced agents have is to position the home and sell at the highest possible price. They have better access to other properties listed

CHAPTER 6: Do You Need an Agent

by other agents.

Like I noted earlier about how good real estate negotiate, going through an agent for a deal is what most people don't like, they believe that direct negotiation between buyer and seller is more transparent. This might be true that the buyer and the seller are in a transaction and they might get along with each other. But this is not always an easy relationship between the buyer and the seller. What happens when you can't handle a contract?

More reason why you need an agent, they deal with contracts on a regular basis and conditions that can be used. A buyer and seller can work together but at the same time they should seek legal counsel. Not everybody can save money.

Buyers who search for homeowners so as to buy from them may not get an agent involve believing that they can save money. However, if only the buyer and the seller can agree to share the savings, they can both save the commission.

Chapter 7
How to Find Deals

We have a lot of things, but we need to find deals at the right place and the right steps to guide through. The most important thing is to be very good as a real estate home flipper. Also, you need to find good deals. One of the tips for finding deals can be from completely useless and damaging to invaluable and priceless, therefore, there would be a need to vet for finding deals that borough you prior to make moves.

CHAPTER 7: How to Find Deals

The more deals you have, the more opportunities you have to get good deals you have.

It's all a game of numbers. So, when you have a long list of homeowners, you would get a higher chance of willing home sellers. So, what this means is that you have to be willing to get all out and contact as many people as possible.

It may take you 10 to 20 emails to find just one prospect. The more homeowners you get in touch with, the greater the chances that someone might want to work with you. Basically, put your head down and straight, the move on the next one, it will eventually get a little easier. Obviously, this means you will have to develop a thick skin.

Rejection is normal in the real estate industry.

Get ready to be rejected. Actually, expect to be rejected. Don't let anyone, not just anyone, I mean negative people influence how hard you work. Definitely, you would meet up with homeowners who are frustrated by their current financial situations. These people may even decide to throw their frustrations at you. See this as a transfer of aggression. It's about them not you. So, they would have transferred aggression at anybody else.

Just don't stop at success.

Just ramp your actions instead of you to stop what you're doing. Keep your pipeline filled as a successful real estate business. Make points, stay consistent and keep at what you're doing. Divide your time, minimize your time every day, every week to get new deals, regardless of what's going on. Don't slow down.

Don't be scared, make enough offers.

New investors aren't successful at finding deals because they don't make enough offers. Not just an offer but an offer that would be comfortable for you, no one plans to do an offer and lose, as much as possible as you can, make better and reasonable offer. Targeting the right properties makes you feel comfortable making offer. It is left to them to reject it if they want to. Unless a seller makes an offer, you will never know what the seller will say.

Most deals are obtained through perseverance and a unique ability outside the box.

Do your research by being proactive and find truly motivated owners who are willing to work with you as you're also willing to work with them. Put in time for this, deals won't just fall into your hand, do little things that would give out real deals.

When you focus on following task, good deals and rehab deals can be found in any market.

A lot of people get confused about these things because they are targeting the wrong people. Why not target vacant properties, disgruntled sellers that are late on their mortgage. Rather than you are focusing on large list and expensive marketing, narrow your focus.

CHAPTER 7: How to Find Deals

Competition will reduce, due spending time and not getting a prospect on time.

If there won't be good deals for finding deals, there wouldn't be a flip show on TV. There are lot of ways to find deals that suits your personality, and also your deals can be done any way you like it. I'm sore you would have found a successful finding deals with the tips listed above.

Deals can be found in different ways but let's take a look at what we have here in details.

On Market Deals

This means deals listed on the MLS (Multiple Listing Service). You can get deals by using MLS an organization that operates a database of properties listing in a given area. They post what they have online for buyers who has access to the MLS. It helps agents and brokers to share information and services and also to market their listing to a wonderful audience. You would be thinking why it is not open to the public, yes, because it is owned and operated by brokers. MLS tends to grant access only to its own due-paying members.

Shopping on MLS for deals is that you're competing against other investors and retail buyers too which steers up prices and makes it much more difficult to find deals that could make a profit.

Let's see how we can use MLS (Multiple Listing Service) to find great deals. A lot of people are willing to list their properties on MLS because they know that, that's the best place where all the retail buyers shop for their houses and all. MLS can be totally competitive for you to buy a property if you're trying to get a potential deal.

Meeting agents should happen in real estate investment and other rehabbers in the market that can be a potential source of leads. Let us take an example of a seller that has a distressed, divorced and family issue, the seller would not want to deal with the dispute of listing their properties on MLS. In cases like this, the seller may contact an area estate agent to negotiate an off-market purchase with a local rehabber that would offer cash for the property and close it quickly.

How you can access the MLS?

Before accessing MLS, you would need to become an agent, this will grant you fill right and access once you get your license. approval for MLS is a formality. But getting this license would take 3 to 5 months and would also cost you $500 - $1000.

Now you might have got access to the MLS, then partner with an agent if you don't have money to become an agent yourself. You may also consider bringing an agent to partner with you in your venture. Having an agent on your team may increase your chances.

You might have a long-standing relationship with the MLS and also get a feed as non-agent, you would likely present a transparent business model and explain in detail how you plan to use the MLS data. You would also need to sign up as an assistant meanwhile some MLS allows

CHAPTER 7: How to Find Deals

unlicensed real estate professionals to have their own MLS account if you provide some service to a local agent, you might ask them to sponsor you for MLS access as their assistant.

A few companies syndicate listing from several MLS and offer them for sale for marketing purposes. One of the most popular List Hub. You can get an MLS data feed if you have the time to become a publisher with one of these syndication services.

If MLS doesn't have its own public-facing website, you may check out some of your local agents and choose a good IDX site. What is an IDX site? It's a website that is managed by an individual agent that includes MLS listing for marketing purposes.

Make use of a data company: sometimes people who think they really need this MLS actually do not need it. There are lots of real estate data out that are not limited to the MLS. Examples of the data available include building permits, owner and buyers, current and past purchase figures, assessed value and property taxes.

Making use of MLS is for you to find deals that would help you have a number of successful deals in flipping houses, with the following guide that's listed above to put you through.

If you live in a strong and good area in a hot market, you can actually forget about finding an amazing flip deal on the (multiple listing service) MLS. But in most competitive markets, you may not find great flip deals where everybody else is looking.

How exactly do you find a good deal? Well, you have to be creative because most people use wholesalers (people who are experts in finding real estate deals for cash buyers) and others use the internet.

Off Market Deals

Deals that cannot be found on MLS marketplace which can be so hard to find but it has less competition, so you can happily buy properties at discount. More hustle, more off market deals but always the best that provides you a profit ability.

As a new investor you would spend time running comps, data to figure out if the home you're looking for is at priced at market value, below market and what you should offered make profit.

You might drive for dollars which can actually be one of the best strategies for finding deals that takes a lot of time and effort. The process of driving for dollars is searching for properties that looked abandoned which could be owned by a seller who is motivated to sell. Now that you may find the property of your choice as a good deal, the property that qualifies, just leave a business postcard at the door, not down the address and write a letter to the property. Make a research of their contact information where you can find the forty owners name on the county recorder's website.

Again, this could take a lot of time, effort and money, like I stated

CHAPTER 7: How to Find Deals

earlier, but in other to find off-market deals that no one else knows about, you will have to do things that nobody else wants to do.

Networking at Real Estate Investment Group meetings can be a great way to meet agents, wholesalers & even other rehabbers in the market that can be a potential source of leads. You don't want to be driving all overlooking for deals the you should down your search to a farm area of just a few neighborhoods so as to help you find those hidden gems. Your network is your worth!

As a beginner to go with the flow, you can try marketing to motivated sellers to find properties to flip. Let me share with you how I discovered my first flip deal that earned me over $25,000, as an apprentice? I make use of direct mail marketing, which is right and sent out letters and postcards to absentee landlords in my target market outline which took an initial investment of about $1000, at first it was a risk. But it really paid off. The reality is that amazing flip deals.

Make use of direct mail to targeted lists of people that might want to sell their properties, Pay Per Click (PPC) Google AdWords advertising and a variety of other methods to find the properties that is flipped.

Let's Talk About Lead Generation

Lead generation is key in finding and purchasing potential investment houses, which means you're going to have to learn this if you will be successful in your real estate venture.

In lead generation, you will have to create a system that works to keep the flow of information for potential investment houses coming, else, you may end up finding no properties to buy.

Leads could be a phone number, contact with a homeowner or with someone who knows a homeowner, an address or a name.

So how do you generate leads? I'll show you. Fundamentally, there are three ways to generate leads; they are prospecting, advertising, and networking.

- **Prospecting:** It is simply examining your target neighborhoods, advertisements or lists that contain potentials for a good investment house. Simply put, prospecting is searching for opportunities. You could simply inspect your target neighborhood in search of a house that is ideal enough to meet your potential investment house criteria. Sometimes, you may just go in search of a "For Sale".

  Other methods of prospecting include MLS, searching for advertisements for sale in the newspapers or on the internet or look out for auctions. If you're searching on the internet, you could use keywords like handyman special, undervalue, estate sale, motivated seller, repair allowance, and so on.

  When you find a house, or houses that fit what you're looking for, go in search of the owner of the property. A few signs that the homeowner may be willing to sell is an old fencing, worn -

out gates, cluttered entryways, untidy lawn or surroundings, no lights when it's dark, and so on.

If you're able to get the contact of the owner, probably through the neighbors, go ahead and contact them by sending an email or putting a call through.

The owner of the property becomes a lead.

- **Advertising:** This method is probably less time-consuming compared to prospecting. Here, the goal is to reach out to sellers through advertisements. It could be done via social media, direct emailing or signs at strategic areas.

In the information you will be passing out, be sure to add that you're exactly what they want, and they can sell their houses quickly, with fast payments.

Create an awareness in your target neighborhood so that property owners there are aware that they can easily reach you if they ever need to sell off their houses. When crafting the message, you will be advertising, be sure that it has the ability to catch the attention of everyone, especially your ideal customer.

You're targeted at someone who is terribly in need of cash and will overlook the value of his house and accept your price. He/she is usually in a haste to be relieved of mortgage payments. Your message should be focused on what the customer stands to gain, for example, a fast deal with quick payments, cash payment upfront and so on. Be clever while crafting this message, make sure that whoever does see it keeps it in mind and even remembers to tell someone about it. Also, try to keep your message as precise as possible and then end with a call to action. An example of a catchy message is," Take a break from the mortgage. Sell your house for fast cash now!", or "So much debt? Reach me, and I'll buy your house hassle-free".

Be as original and as fun as you can be, but if you can't be fun, then I suggest you go straight to the point. But make sure there's a call to action. You can use a bulletin, a billboard, T-shirts, direct mail, banners, flyers, business cards, company newsletters, door hangers, the internet, newspapers, TV or radio to send out your message.

When Wrigly was asked why he continued to advertise his chewing gums even when it was already all over the market, here's what Wrigly had to say, "Simple. Sales is a train, and advertising is the engine. Cut the engine off and the train will eventually come to a halt".

A homeowner who reaches you as a result of your advertisement becomes a lead.

- **Networking:** This is probably the easiest way to generate leads. Here, you'll simply establish a connection with individuals who could bring you leads and opportunities. While establishing a connection, let everyone who matters know that you are an investor and you're looking for properties to buy.

It could be a family member, a real estate agent, an old school mate or a friend, they will most likely call you up when they

CHAPTER 7: How to Find Deals

have something for you.

I would suggest that you be more strategic in your networking. The people you're establishing a connection with should be people who have professions that place them directly in contact with houses or homeowners. While doing this, be sure that you're also of use to the other person to strengthen the relationship.

Keep in mind that in networking, your reputation is important. You want to be seen as trustworthy and thoughtful, try to be gracious and as generous as you can. Consider the seeds of your actions that will eventually cause returns.

A good place to start networking is in real estate investment clubs. Here, you will find lenders, builders, investors. Appraisers, and so on. You will also need accountants, lawyers, inspectors, contractors, builders and residents at your target neighborhood. Then try to remain in regular contact with them.

If you're up to the task, you could use all three lead generation methods.

What Happens When You Get a Lead?

It is important to note that not every lead will be useful to you. You will, therefore, have to set up criteria for measuring the qualification of a lead. Two major criteria are required to qualify a lead as useful:

- The seller must be willing to sell below market value.
- The house must meet your buying criteria

INVESTING IN REAL ESTATE: Flipping Houses

If a lead does not meet these criteria, discard and move on. Try not to go about checking every lead as you will be wasting a lot of time. It's best you speak with the homeowner first and ask all the questions you need before qualifying the lead.

Remember to pass on a lead that is not useful to you to another investor in your network, it may be useful to them.

Chapter 8
How to Find an Ideal Property

The easiest part of this business is watching it on TV, that easy part is what happen after you buy the house. It's important to look at any property objectively before you get too excited about a new deal. When

INVESTING IN REAL ESTATE: Flipping Houses

analyzing a deal, you need to be sure to look at both the best and the worst-case scenarios, so you don't end up purchasing properties with too much risk.

How can you identify a good investment house?

- It needs to be fixed up.
- It is in a desirable part of town
- The owner of the property is willing to sell at a cheaper rate.

Look into previously owned homes: occupying a home from previous owner or a real agent. Foreclosure properties might fall under the categories of previously owned homes and current market is full of foreclosure properties which are often up to 70% below.

When searching for a house to flip, buy an old house in a highly respected or upcoming neighborhood. The homes in these neighborhoods would have been priced above so when you completely renovate them with new appliances and structural repairs, you will sell for even more and here you are with a successful flipping.

Look for houses that have a solid foundation and structure, but have 'undesirable' features: ugly paint, old windows, unkempt lawns, old furniture and so on. These things are easy to fix and can lower your price, better still, inspect the house, consider bringing an agent to avoid houses with big problems Avoid properties with major problems such as a leaky roof or plumbing systems in need of repair which would cost you a lot of money.

Tips to Consider before Purchasing an Investment Property

Now we will turn our attention to some essential tips that top house flippers in the industry use and implement when they flip houses. When you're aware of these tips, you'll be able to use them as you move through the research and purchasing process of buying a property to flip. Let's take a look at some of these essential tips now.

Tip 1: Work within Your Budget

As you become more comfortable with calculating your ARV, you should also become more comfortable with calculating how much money you're going to spend on your property. Once you have an average number in mind that you're willing to spend, you need to make sure that you work within this number. So many new investors fall in love with a certain property, and then try to make this purchase a reality by reallocating funds and sacrificing money in other areas of their life. It would be best if you worked to avoid doing this. Once you have your budget set, stick to it. This means that even if you find a house that you fall in love with, if it's out of your budget, you need to walk away. As you move through this process, it's important to remember that you're looking for a property to flip, not a property that you need to love because, ideally, this house is not for you. Keep your emotions at bay, and you'll be one step closer to finding investment property success.

Tip 2: Choose the Right Neighborhood

Within the real estate realm, there are typically three types of neighborhoods that exist on the market. These neighborhoods are labeled rather simply as "A," "B," and "C." Let's take a look at each neighborhood type now, so you can see which type of neighborhood you should be looking to purchase a house within:

- **Neighborhood A**: Neighborhood A is a neighborhood that is comprised of primarily single-family homes. These neighborhoods can be best described as the ones that you might see in an affluent neighborhood. An example of this type of neighborhood includes a gated community or a community made up of making six figures, having two children, and having someone who cuts their lawn every week. There are not many renters in these types of communities.
- **Neighborhood B**: This type of neighborhood can be described as a working-class neighborhood. When you go through this type of neighborhood, you will likely see work trucks and vans in the driveways. Another sign that you're in a type B neighborhood is that there are duplexes and multi-family homes scattered throughout the neighborhood.
- **Neighborhood C**: This type of neighborhood is one that is rather run-down and neglected. In a C type neighborhood, there is a

greater chance that the tenants of this home could eventually be in a position where they are unable to pay their rent. This would leave you in the unfortunate situation of having a vacant property.

Neighborhood type B is the best type of neighborhood to invest in when you're looking to flip a house. Of course, if you are someone who is a professional contractor and know that you can turn a home that needs fixing up into a home that can contend within an A-type neighborhood, more power to you; however, for many new house flippers, this is not reality. A B type neighborhood will offer you more of an opportunity to be as flexible as possible with your exit strategy. In this type of neighborhood, the neighbors will probably be the most accepting of your presence in their community.

Tip 3: Keep Size in Mind

For inexperienced house flippers, I would advise you to start small and build up from there. I can actually say my biggest mistakes must have come from taking on projects that were too big, avoid big projects that won't make you sell the house just to realize how bad the deal would be.

This tip is pretty simple. When you're looking to flip your first property, you want to make sure that you're keeping the size of your project in mind. Why would you take on a colossal house when you have never taken on this kind of work before? Start smaller, and if you enjoy the work that you're doing, you can gradually work up to flipping homes that are large and will afford you a greater profit.

Tip 4: Be Cautious of the Short Sale

When a homeowner decides that it's a good idea to stop paying his or her mortgage payments for one reason, the bank will foreclose on the property. This is a hassle for the bank because it essentially takes on the debt that the homeowner had previously owned. Often, if there is still debt left to be paid to the bank against the property, the bank will try to sell it at a discounted rate because there is less to be paid off than there would be in a typical mortgage.

While this may seem like a great situation that you can take advantage of from an investment perspective, the bank will avoid selling you a home at a discounted rate if they can help it. This being the case, it can often take a much longer time for the bank to release this property to you, which means that you will be waiting around to start doing work on it and flipping it.

Additionally, a good short sale is going to be bought quickly by another experienced and savvy property investor. While it might be a good idea to start learning more about how short sales work when starting, it might be a good idea to avoid them.

The Importance of Targeting Neighborhoods

The first step is looking out for a neighborhood that has a selling potential. Simply put, these are neighborhoods with "investment houses".

Targeting neighborhoods will help you direct your resources more specifically in order to land good investment property leads. Plus, it is time and energy consuming being all over the place when you could just work on a more direct approach for the best possible results.

Here are a few reasons why targeting neighborhoods is important:

- It saves so much time
- A lower cost for each qualified lead, so you don't have to spend resources on undesirable choices.
- You find ideal properties faster than you would have if your choice was more spread out.
- In little time, you may become an expert in your chosen neighborhood which could generate even more leads and help you assess prices better.

How to Identify a Good Target Neighborhood

When I say, "good target neighborhood", take your mind off the hustle and bustle of big neighborhoods, it isn't always assessed that way.

A good target neighborhood is one that has a fast value-increase.

Let me explain; you see, we know that the value of a property automatically improves after a rehabilitation. However, you would be a poor investor if that's all you rely on for value appreciation.

The most important thing you need to look out for in a neighborhood is potential.

I'll show you how to do this in six simple ways:

- Carry out your research on the price range of existing properties in the neighborhood
- Check its proximity to your home, school or workplace.
- Find out how old the other properties in the neighborhood are.
- Don't leave out the aesthetics of the neighborhood. How desirable is it?
- Is this neighborhood safe?
- Put into consideration, the sales activity of other properties in the neighborhood.

Price Range of Existing Properties

It's common sense to know that getting an expensive house and fixing it up improves its potential of being sold for even more money. The same goes for getting a cheap house and fixing it up. Of course, it would require more capital to buy a home and fix it up. All of that would certainly take time, coupled with the responsibilities that come along like tax, interest, insurance, and so on. The worst decision you would make is spending so much time and money on a neighborhood and then realizing later that the average price of a property in the area is way beyond your budget and ability.

It would best to go for properties in a neighborhood with an average price that is affordable according to your ability and budget so that fixing up and handling the other expenses will not cost you much. Plus,

CHAPTER 8: How to Find an Ideal Property

you want to go about this in such a way that you still have a margin of profit that would make the risk worth it.

Proximity to Home, Workplace or School

I've already mentioned how time-consuming this venture is. It's crucial to find effective ways to save as much time as you can. In the case of choosing a neighborhood, you want a somewhere that is easily accessible from your home or workplace.

Since you will have to visit your investment house often, a neighborhood that is quite a distance from you will make it difficult to keep your eyes on the fixing up process, and if you do keep an eye, your time and money will go into just moving to and for; not good.

If, however, you have lots of free town to keep tabs on an investment house located really far away, then, by all means, go for it. But this isn't advisable if you do not have the luxury, you will need to be involved in the rehab of the investment house full-time.

Age of the Properties

It's essential to find out the age of properties in the neighborhood as it could be a huge advantage for you. The older the established neighborhood is, the higher the owner equity of houses located there will be.

As a result, the owner of the house may be more willing to sell off the house to you at a value that is below market value, since they would've paid a good part of the mortgage. A house that is still new would have no need for improvement, which could mean little value appreciation and low owner equity.

While we're at it, I should add that the age of the property will not always work in your favor. There's the need to consider how much it would cost to fix the place up. It would generally cost less to fix up a twenty-five or a thirty-year-old house than it would to fix up one that is above a hundred years. This is because, for all older houses, you may need a total overhaul of the plumbing, the kitchen, wiring, flooring, and so on.

Ultimately, while targeting a neighborhood by its age, pay attention to the exact age, try not to go for one that would cost more than your budget for a fix-up. Also look out for signs that the house is aging, like old and discolored painting, a roofing that is falling apart, old fencing, and so on.

These boost your improvement opportunities. In all, keep the risk of an over-the-top cost of rehabilitation and the benefit of a high owner equity, so that you do not end up at a loss.

Neighborhood Desirability

The aesthetics of a neighborhood is another important factor in determining your target neighborhood. You should be sure it is a neighborhood someone would want to live in.

People generally want a neighborhood that is close to schools,

CHAPTER 8: How to Find an Ideal Property

recreational places, offices, stores and has a good reputation.

See it this way, if there were two houses with same features but in different neighborhoods, say one is in a more desirable neighborhood compared to the other, do you think they would both go for the same price? Good.

Safety

On safety, I'm speaking of both your safety and that of the potential buyer. Since you will spend a mighty number of hours there and may be leaving late at night, you want a neighborhood that you do not feel threatened in, when it's dark.

An unsafe neighborhood will make you become not as active in the rehabilitation process, and one day that you are present, you will itch to leave on time, consequently being almost uninvolved in the fix-up process of the investment house. Plus, if your potential buyers are aware of the safety problems of the neighborhood, then they may become disinterested.

Sales Activity

The sales activity of properties in the neighborhood is an important factor to consider before buying the house. Have you noticed that houses often sell faster in some neighborhoods while others remain empty for months before finally getting sold?

The areas with faster sales are good target neighborhoods and it would be wise to get an investment house there. The sales activity may be affected by the desirability of the neighborhood, the age, taxes, amenities, features, and so on.

To evaluate the sales activity, check for how many houses are for sale, how many sold the past year and how long each property took to be sold. This will help determine the sales activity of the properties in the neighborhood.

Qualify the house

For the house to meet your criteria, you will have to find out a few things. A house that you do not like should be abandoned. This is what your criteria should look like:

- For starters, it should be in your target neighborhood.
- Then, check that the necessary repairs are not more than your budget can take.
- The house should not be too different from others in the neighborhood as this can be a turnoff for buyers. Examples of unique issues include crime scene, too close to the highway, and so on.

You can ask the seller these questions and then take your cue from there. If you would prefer to see the house yourself, then by all means, do so.

Next, Qualify the Seller

A qualified seller is one who is willing to sell the house for less than the market value. This is only possible if they have the motivation and the means to sell the house.

A homeowner has the means if he/she has equity and cash to pay off any loans. A homeowner is motivated to sell below market value if they need to sell the house fast, without hassles. Other motivations could be financial troubles, certain unfortunate or fortunate occurrences like a disability, death, divorce, job transfer, and so on or unwillingness to fix things up around the house.

When you have ascertained that the seller is qualified, you will need to determine how much you can give the seller for the house after going over and taking a look at the property. We will call this "The House Analysis".

The House Analysis

A proper house analysis is the next step after ascertaining that the house and the seller are qualified according to your criteria.

You may be thinking you've successfully gone past the difficult stage, but you see, every stage is going to be just as difficult as the last, including the house analysis stage. If you ever get to this stage, Kudos! You've done well for yourself, but this is probably where the real work begins.

The House Analysis has got to be the most important step; it literally determines the success of everything that comes after it, from the profit potential of the investment house, to the cost spent on rehabilitation to how successfully your reselling goes.

- It is at this stage that we can tell if you will make money or lose money.
- You will, therefore, have to decide the maximum offer you can make for the property after looking through, while making sure that the offer you're making is a smart one.
- Keep in mind the repair costs so that you do not end up making a careless offer.
- You need to know your maximum offer so that you can see when the deal is too risky, when your emotions are getting in the way and when a deal is unprofitable.
- You will have to be timely while doing your calculations so that you do not lose the potential opportunity.

Here's how to go about it. Start by knowing the selling price of the house, that is, the price the house can eventually be sold after fixing it up.

But How Do You Determine the Selling Price?

The first rule of thumb is to never overestimate the selling price of a property. You will have to learn to read and interpret the market or hire a professional to help. You can do it yourself by doing the following:

Mind the MLS so that you come up with a comparative market analysis

CHAPTER 8: How to Find an Ideal Property

report of the other properties recently sold in the neighborhood. Your real estate agent can help you do this. The details (layout, age, size, and so on.) of the houses in the neighborhood should be the same as the one you have your attention on.

Next, go to the sites of these neighboring properties to get a visual inspection so you confirm that you're not making a mistake. Use the condition of the adjacent properties, the aesthetics i.e. lawn, architecture, landscaping, and so on, proximity to establishments like a transport station, a railroad, a mall, bus stops, power lines, and so on.., to compare your potential investment house and the other neighboring properties so that you're sure you're not overpricing or underpricing.

Pay attention to the market, as the market environment is a huge determinant in predicting the property's ESP. You want to know what the mortgage rate trends are, the buying cycle.

Look for a potential of development between your buying period and your selling period. A more developed place means a higher ESP. A good way to tell is to check what the other neighborhoods are up to.

Ask experts (the appraisers, the neighborhood specialist real estate agents and the neighborhood residents), their knowledge just could save your life (and your pocket).

House Inspection

Now the type of house you're buying, does it meet your requirement:

INVESTING IN REAL ESTATE: Flipping Houses

- Firstly, make a list of the kind of property with must have, have the list at hand and cross check it as you tour properties around, and if you've decided to found a home that suit your findings, double check it again and again before going for it.
- Have you checked out the area? Is it not going to have flood issues during raining season? Is it close to places you can get things easily? So, I would suggest you take a drive down before you submit an offer. The location most people would most likely prefer will be a place that has an easy access to school, restaurant, shopping and place of worship. You shouldn't choose the right house. Choose the right neighborhood!
- The number of the bedroom is determining. Moreover, the style of the bedroom and bed size matters too.
- The kitchen setup isn't left out too, yeah, I can call this the heart of a home where the families gather here for a great meal, we can also call it a center of activity, be specific about how large or small it should be. Most people don't like a very big kitchen and vice versa and also whether to decide if a store can be at the corner of the kitchen or outside close to the kitchen.
- Make a check of the appliances, they can be so expensive to replace.
- Have you managed to check the roof? Rather would prefer you check through before going in to see the construction of the house, confirm if the roof is caving in or new? And avoid a home that would cost you much. When you step inside, focus on the

CHAPTER 8: How to Find an Ideal Property

structural part and naked wire. Keep it in mind that when choosing the type of house, you should buy houses that won't cost you much on heating and cooling system.

- Test the plumbing by running the shower, opening the taps, check for the sink in the kitchen, the leaks, the toilet, and the kitchen pipes. Investigate and look through the area, check the surroundings because it can't be left out. Any unpleasant smell? Sewage system can get clogged by tree roots, fortunately, some plumbing companies would suggest that they make use of the camera through the pipes to detect any blockages or break.
- Also check out the little details such as, turning on and turning off the switch, opening and closing the windows and doors. Literally, get your hands on everything, taste the water, flush the toilet. People tends to focus on the cost of cabinet, appliances and so on but most times they forget the cost of labor which can double up the cost. Basically, you should factor in those cost when you're deciding whether you can afford it.
- You can also check if there's parking space, if there's traffic on the street and also go during rainy season.

Have a home inspection done, make sure you enlist a professional to help you look into the foundation if it's solid, and the wiring up is well fixed. You can take pictures and videos of each house to help you recollect each home, tour homes with your price range and most likely taking notes of this things might be helpful.

Mind you, when buying a house there are papers to sign. Contracts are

INVESTING IN REAL ESTATE: Flipping Houses

meant to be negotiated, there's no need for signing a standard agreement if you want more time to review your inspection. It requires patience and time to find the right home.

Finalize your ESP

Next, remove how much it would cost to carry out a rehabilitation. This means you will need to do an estimate while checking for the faults so that you know exactly what you're fixing without leaving anything out. You will need to pay attention to details to pull this off.

Try to not overlook or underestimate any detail while doing so. Your seller may chip in how "insignificant" something is, do not fall for it, or else, you may end up paying for part of your rehabilitation cost with your profit. While doing all of this, remember that you will have to be fast so that you can close the deal because, in the heat of the competitiveness, you may lose your seller. Add the cost of hiring labor, or you could hire a contractor who would be in charge of the entire rehabilitation process, they end up handling the calculation of the rehabilitation cost. If you're concerned about making a mistake, it's best you hire a professional to help.

Afterwards, determine the cost associated with the buying, holding and reselling. This is often known as the quiet costs, quiet as they may often be ignored.

Quiet costs may round up to about fifteen percent of the ESP. Quiet cost is made up of the buying, holding, money and selling cost. Costs incurred when you buy a house is known as buying cost. This includes an appraisal, title insurance, survey, inspection, and documentation. Holding costs occur during the period you become the house owner. This includes insurance, tax, maintenance, utility. Money costs are the expenses that come with borrowed money for the venture. They often depend on the borrowed amount, the agreed duration, terms& conditions. Selling costs include costs that come with the sale of the house. This majorly includes the commission for your real estate agent and the closing costs.

Take out the amount you want as profit from that particular venture, putting into consideration the risk potential.

What you have left is the maximum offer.

Make an Offer

Make an offer which helps you understand how to make an attractive offer. Get an agent who can help you prepare a complete offer package including your proof of funds for down payment, offer price and pre-approval letter.

Get recommendations for inspection of home from your agents and be sure you do your findings before choosing one, you would need to complete a home inspection 10 - 15 days after you've signed a purchase agreement.

INVESTING IN REAL ESTATE: Flipping Houses

You would be responsible to pay the home inspector as a buyer, while the fees vary, you might pay an average of $250 - $500. Just be sure that your home inspector has enough experience, and also read online n take time to read reviews, ask for past clients references and check out their credentials.

Your final approval loans you need to keep your finance and during underwriting you should credit in line. It takes couple of days to complete the financing process, and also delay may be caused by slow response of disclosure from buyers and exact documents are not provided. Respond to request to double check your loan.

Chapter 9

Financial Analyses of a Potential Deal

Having factored your expenses, there will be room for profits to know what the house can sell for. Following the steps to analyze your deal will help you fix and flip right.

INVESTING IN REAL ESTATE: Flipping Houses

1. Knowing the After-Repair Value

What the home will worth once it's fixed and also in a good condition is the after repair after value. You may wish to have your realtor run the sale matching using the MLS which they have access to as licensed agents. They help you find the features you requested for such as the number of bedrooms, a story building or two, number of bathrooms and homes recently sold with less similar features. There might be a need for your homes to see the level of finishing so as to stop you from overdoing the rehab.

You need to stay within your budget so as to enable you to make a profit. And if rehab exceeds this budget, then the property won't work out then you will have to search for another investment property.

2. Your Profit Expectation

Your expected profit is an important cost to factor. It is important to analyze your investment to make you stick to your required profit and to be sure if the deal will work or probably not for you. Profit will differ when you overestimate your budget.

3. Closing Stocks

If you're using leverage to cover expenses that your loan isn't covering, you would be required to bring money. Otherwise, if you're not using loan then you will make use of cash due to closing stocks that vary but

CHAPTER 9: Financial Analyses of a Potential Deal

include:

- Loan fee, lenders charge loan originating fee to process the loan paperwork.
- A fee for running your credit report will be charged, this can be an attorney's fees.
- Discount points, an exchange for a lower interest rate.
- Documenting fee, this is basically for new land records.
- Insuring fee and title search fees.

4. Closing Costs

You will have several expenses to pay once you've decided to sell your property. Real estate commission is charged 7% which is the expenses you pay.

If you decide to sell a home yourself, there's a need for you to hire a realtor to sell your home, with the benefits that include marketing, access to their network of potential buyers, legal work and more. To ensure that the property title is clear and ready to the next owner without any defects you would pay for the title work.

5. Holding Cost

This is an expense category, that requires you to pay for some utilization when you're doing a flip such as electricity, waste removal, water and so on. Expenses might add up if flip takes several months to complete. And if you took out for a loan, you'll have to pay mortgage interest. To sum it up, you should also have in mind to pay for taxes, debt interest, and insurance, with some other holding stock.

Be conservative with your estimates, it's reasonable to be sure about. Saving more money on the flip if the flip went well will boost your profit. Don't purchase more than the price when you're analyzing your deal.

Instead of submitting high offers, why not submit low offers and see what next because the seller may scepter your offer when interested or motivated. There's no way a seller can accept offers if the max price is ridiculous. Instead of looking for a bigger and neat house why not look for outdated homes in order to have a good start with a low offer process.

6. Profit

Your deal is to get home to flip and your aim is to make profit, the profit can be the left-over of the cost from the sale of the property. **The formula for profit** would be:

$$PROFIT = ARV - Project\ Cost$$

On the low edge, the minimum profit you should aim for should be $15,000 - $25,000. Anything less than this amount is in the worst case.

Formula for ROI:

CHAPTER 9: Financial Analyses of a Potential Deal

Do you know what ROI means? Return on Investment, this is a profit from the money used to execute a project.

$$ROI = Profit / Project\ Costs$$

Aiming for 15-25% ROI.

Take note, you shouldn't find yourself in a deal that's the margin is not satisfactory or deals that are risky.

Rate of return (ROR)

Is pertaining to ROI over a period of time. These formulas are helpful to understand the effect on your deals.

$$ROR = ROI / 365\ days$$

The rate of return helps you to know the deal to go after between similar deals.

7. Know Your Budget

The amount of money you can raise to risk a flip. If you've not been able to sell the house is a loss, you're willing to take in the event, find your way to sell the house quickly.

Meet with your agent to check your house price and your rehab project, don't buy a house in a rush to avoid you having less money for upgrading, tell your agent about your budget, so that he can show you houses you can purchase and rehab within your budget. Have you outline your budget?

8. Calculate

The buying, selling and carrying costs for various houses price in your budget, including the down payment, closing cost and agent commission, inspection fee, tax, and interest. When your budget has a full inspection, it reduces the chances of buying a house with a problem that will be discovered immediately the rehab work starts. To rehab costs, set a target budget ratio of a home purchase.

Let's take an example to see how our budget looks like, for example, Let's say you have $20,000 worth of cash for upgrading houses, budget $15,000 to $17000 for the rehab, Be certain to include the calculation of your carrying costs, such as utilities and debt service depending on your projected rehab. To guide your real estate agent in selecting a house, use the amount of money budgeted and tell your agent your profit target for the flip.

You might have decided the house that suits your budget to flip, now you will meet with your contractors to get the cost on the construction work such as roofing, tiles, cabinets, plumbing, toilets, sinks and so

CHAPTER 9: Financial Analyses of a Potential Deal

many other items.

I'm sure by now, you would have an idea of how your budget will look like. So, you have to create your budget documents for different home prices. Now, include your budget balance for rehab cost. Buy a home that has balance of enough money to complete the improvement that will help you sell for a price and gives you your desire profit.

9. Basic Investment

An idea which involves buying and selling fast for a higher price. But the best thing you can do is buying a house at lower price and selling it for a higher price. Get the right property and fix it yourself, be sure it's something you can fix yourself or talk to your agent.

Know that you need to get a financing to start a house flipping project. If your property is not selling right away, you need to absorb the high interest rates, saying that, money is important. Now that people hold onto property for a short time, the high interest was not a big bargain. Sometimes when you calculate in your head thinking it's easy, you may want to do the project yourself, but it requires professional. Before you start renovating, find a local business and estimate.

10. Why You Need to Work with a Designer?

Yes, I am sure you would like a colorful design, beautiful interior, a designer helps you get a nice and long-lasting fabric and color, this would look more attractive to the buyers. But I am sure you know it is not for free, of course, so manage your time looking for designer before renovating.

Well, this business looks easy but not, at the same time is fun and a fast way to earn money within a short period of time. Like I always remind you, make sure you do a proper research and stick to smaller properties with less work before finding your way around to bigger properties so as to gain experience and learning you from your mistakes and your budget increases.

Chapter 10
Negotiation Tips when Buying a House

I once heard George Ross, Donald Trump's lead negotiating attorney, talk about a study done to distinguish the most important trait a great negotiator must possess. If you don't know, George is the secret weapon to Donald's substantial real estate deals. From what I've read, George has negotiated hundreds of millions of deals in the New York area alone, and he's got some great books on putting deals together I highly recommend.

The outcome of this study determined that <u>PERSONALITY</u> is the most important trait that master negotiators possess. That means yes, you're going to have to intelligently hold a conversation with people to negotiate great deals and make any money as well. You must know & understand who you are. As for me, I know I can talk to anybody. It's no problem for me to walk up to a stranger and strike up a conversation. If you can't do that, rest assured I will give you some great lines to ask people that will open them up immediately.

If you have a hard time talking to people, you're going to have to work on that. It may take some time, but it can be mastered. Just like any other art form, it takes practice. Remember, negotiating great deals is an ART form, not a science.

That means 2 different people can approach the same problem in 2 completely different ways and still win. There's no exact 1 way to get the desired outcome when negotiating. You may do this a bit differently than I would but still get the same result. Just like there are 32 teams in the NFL (National Football League), which means 32 different head coaches. Each coach believes he's doing the correct things to get his team to a win. The team owners also think the coaches are doing the right things, or they wouldn't be paying them millions each year. You may talk to a homeowner and say things differently than I would to get

CHAPTER 10: Negotiation Tips when Buying a House

the deal. There is no 1 way to negotiate effectively.

You will need to understand your personality to achieve maximum results. Know who you are. If you need some help figuring that out, take some time to read hip hop Mogul Russell Simons' book "Do YOU." It goes into great detail about how to just be yourself to get what you want out of life. Take some time to accept who you are, so you don't mess up trying to be something you're not.

There are 4 basic things you must remember in a negotiation to be effective. There is an acronym that will help you remember it. That's **POST**

P - Who are the people and the personalities involved?

O - What is the objective of this negotiation?

S - What is Strategy(s) you'll use to win (Game Plan)

T - What tactics will you use to implement Strategy

I wish I could take credit for this, but I will give all credit to George Ross. I believe he's one of the top real estate attorneys of our time. He says you must understand these 4 things to have a good negotiation.

Who are the people and the personalities involved?

Remember, we said personality is the #1 trait great negotiators possess. You'll have to get people to open up and talk to you, so you'll know what their personality is. Are you dealing with a person that only has a few minutes to talk like a busy attorney, or are you dealing with a retired person that can talk all day. You must recognize what type of person is in the negotiation with you. This will allow you to craft your conversation accordingly.

Art that's lacking in this country & in most marriages is LISTENING. When was the last time you sat down and listened to somebody? Perhaps a friend or a spouse without interjecting your thoughts or your opinion and just listening to the other person's problems & what's going on in their life. Giving them your undivided attention and caring about their wellbeing. Learning to be a master listener will allow you to build rapport with sellers and react to their stories better. Truthfully all you're going to do is listen to stories when you visit the house anyway. The real trick is to react to their stories in a way that will make them relate to you & like you. The next step is to ask the correct questions simply, then SHUT UP. This little secret will get you halfway to a great deal.

Is the person you're talking to the owner of the house, or is he a spouse, relative, or friend of the owner. Are there multiple owners that need to sign off to sell or is it just one person on the deed. To be effective, you must know exactly who you're negotiating with. It would be a complete waste of time and skill to apply all that's in this book to a person with no right to sell the house. Yes, it would be great practice, but you can still practice real homeowners.

Are they sad about selling this house or happy to just be getting rid of a problem house they inherited? You'll be able to get a sense of each homeowner's attitude by responding to your questions. Remember,

CHAPTER 10: Negotiation Tips when Buying a House

know what type of personality you're dealing with and how they're related to the house.

What is the key objective of this negotiation?

What is your objective when negotiating with this homeowner? You should always know your exit strategy before you go into a house if you can. Sometimes a person just won't give you all the details over the phone, so you'll have to take a chance. But I recommend knowing how you're going to get out of the house before you go in. Knowing how you're going to get paid is your ultimate exit strategy. This is a huge issue for several flippers. They get so worried about negotiating with sellers that they forget what their objective is.

You must keep your mind in game mode 100% of the time once you pull up to the seller's house. Knowing how you will be exchanging this house for dollars will allow you to be a better negotiator. If you plan to keep the house for rental, then you know you may be able to pay a higher price. If you plan to assign your contract for a quick cash sale, then you know you'll need all the discounts you can find. If you plan to renovate it yourself, you'll have to get your repairs itemized so you know how much to budget.

For this, we are going to focus mainly on the objective of buying at a discount. That means you want the seller to accept a low offer for the house. You will need to focus on that objective the entire time you're at the seller's house. Each question you ask will be moving them 1 step closer to a "yes." Your objective is to first get the seller to like you than getting them to trust you and ultimately signing your paperwork.

TIP: Remember, we never use the word "contract" we always use "paperwork." It has a less life-altering sound to it.

What is Strategy for this negotiation?

There are countless negotiation strategies, techniques & tactics. When you first start talking with a homeowner, you'll be focusing on 1 specific strategy. The strategy is called the PROBLEM-AGITATE-SOLUTION (P-A-S) strategy. You'll need to find out WHY the person is selling their house. This is the main key to getting the deal.

Always remember about intimately understanding why your seller wants to dump their house. If you just don't want to dig deep enough, you would not get the best deals. Knowing why they're selling is my favorite way to negotiate Killer deals. I can just feel my posture rising as I'm setting this technique up, and I know when it's going well. The (P-A-S) technique is extremely powerful, and I want you to memorize this as you read this book and beyond.

This is the Strategy of the master negotiator. We want to:

1. Identify the problem
2. Agitate the problem
3. Offer a solution to the problem (be the solution)

You can use this technique on all of your leads that are truly motivated sellers. It's not as effective with sellers that are not motivated to sell. So,

CHAPTER 10: Negotiation Tips when Buying a House

let's make sure you're talking to the right people. This technique is powerful because the seller doesn't even know you're using this mind game on him. He's backing himself up into a mental corner the entire time you're at the house. The main premise of the P-Strategy is to get the seller talking so you can find out the problem (the reason for selling). Next, you need to make the seller talk about his problem in great detail.

TIP: Trying to use the (Problem-Agitate-Solution) strategy on sellers that merely want to sell instead of needing to sell will not be effective. If you try to break this rule, you may get somebody extremely mad at you!

What tactics will you use to implement Strategy?

The sellers we'll be negotiating with are usually suffering from a problem house. Our tactic will be the best way to introducing the problem to the homeowner.

We usually don't want just to come out and say, "Hey, you've got an ugly house, and you need to sell it." There are ways to walk the seller down the path to allow them to see their problem without you having to point it out to them.

We may use different tactics depending on the personality of our seller. Perhaps we need to be direct and ask them about the repairs. Or maybe we'll walk through the house with the seller and simply place our feet in a soft spot on the floor and stand there for a while to wait for a response. Or sometimes, we may just look at a brown spot in the ceiling to see what the seller will say when we look in that direction.

You'll be the judge whether to be direct or use more nonverbal signals to get the seller talking about their problem house.

The 100-10-1 Rule

Discovering extraordinary deals to put resources into is the most troublesome and most significant piece of real estate contributing. Experienced real estate investors comprehend that they make their benefit when they buy the property, not when they sell it.

Every property has various qualities that must be inspected, and one explicit issue with the property may wind up being a major issue that powers the speculator to continue looking. One disregarded insight regarding the property can transform the anticipated benefit into a sizable misfortune.

Many real estate investors subscribe to the "100:10:3:1 rule" or "100:10:1" rule:

- A real estate investor must glance at 100 properties to discover 10 potential deals that can be gainful.
- From these 10 potentials deals a financial specialist will submit offers on 3.
- Of the 3 offers submitted, 1 will be acknowledged.

Finding an appropriate venture property opportunity is a very tedious

CHAPTER 10: Negotiation Tips when Buying a House

procedure, however the exertion is totally important to locate the correct property that will deliver a strong return.

Lost Deals = Lost Profits

Imagine a scenario where the real estate investor doesn't get the "1" and loses it to rivalry. Inability to make sure about the "1" deal after the colossal measure of time and exertion expected to discover quality open doors can be a huge misuse of a speculator's assets and significant loss of potential benefits.

Passing up 3-4 great deals for each year could make the financial specialist miss out on $75,000-$500,000+ of benefit every year. In the event that the speculator can't secure the great deals they discover, why burn through the hour of searching for them in any case?

Don't Get involved in a Bidding War

Essentially offering the most noteworthy sum for the property isn't the appropriate response. Expanding the offer may improve the probability of having the merchant acknowledge the offer, yet every extra dollar offer by the investor is a dollar that comes straight out of the investor's benefit. An offering war will rapidly take the potential undertaking from gainful to a venture that will simply make back the initial investment or more awful.

In what manner can the investor rapidly secure the property without basically expanding the offer and paying more? The investor must separate their idea from the opposition by introducing an offer that outcomes in the seller getting their cash as fast and effectively as could be expected under the circumstances.

Offer with Cash

Trying to offer all cash is a choice that will catch the merchant's eye. No financing possibilities and a simpler, brisk close. In any case, tying up an enormous part of the investor's capital in one property may keep the investor from having the option to act rapidly on another open door around the bend.

On the off chance that the property being bought will be rehabbed, the investor must save enough capital close by for development costs and a hold subsidize in the event that something goes wrong. At whatever point conceivable, it's ideal to keep an adequate measure of cash in the financial balance.

Offer using Hard Money Financing

An idea with a hard cash advance isn't as solid as an idea with all cash, however it very well may be the following best thing. Hard cash enables the investor to close rapidly and the adaptability to keep more cash on hard. Numerous hard cash banks can support in 5-10 days and require an initial installment of around 25%.

An accomplished merchant (or encountered vender's specialist) comprehends that hard cash credits are financed a lot quicker than ordinary bank advances. A hard cash moneylender is additionally less inclined to locate some little insight concerning the exchange ultimately

CHAPTER 10: Negotiation Tips when Buying a House

and pull out of financing the deal (something banks are known to do once in a while).

While a full cash offer is regularly the most ideal approach to make sure about a property at a decent cost when there is rivalry, it's an extravagance not many investors can bring to the table. What's more, the results of passing up future deals while the cash is tied up in the present task could likewise end up being expensive.

At the point when a cash offer is absurd, or the investor wishes to save enough assets available for another potential venture, a hard cash advance might be the best alternative for offering a brisk close and separating themselves from the opposition to make sure about their current "1" property.

Mistakes Not to Do while Making Offers

You might probably have room for negotiation where homes are tends to stay longer in the buyer's market, and sometimes it is uncommon for multiple buyers to oppose the same property which may not let you have enough chance to negotiate all.

Focusing on the sales price as a buyer is good, because you're submitting to pay it off by submitting the offer. Moreover, consider the type of market you're into. Also take not that it's bad to keep a buyer waiting for too long. Resist the trick to cover up yourself by electing as

INVESTING IN REAL ESTATE: Flipping Houses

many contingencies as possible as you put your offer together.

You shouldn't fail to get a pre-approved for a mortgage: Determine how much you can afford and get a pre-approved house for a mortgage. This pre-approved letter is a confirmation that you will be eligible to borrow the amount needed base on the lender's evaluation of your assets and income.

Does pre-approval take so long? Yes, it takes longer and needs an application, it's worthwhile investment.

There's something that can damage your credibility which is, if a bank is willing to give you a loan of $300,000 doesn't mean you should accept the offer for $300,000 be wise and don't let it damage your credibility. There are more homes to meet your needs and wants.

Don't be greedy while making offer: negotiating can be a mistake when you're being too greedy even when nobody is ready to leave the table when there's nothing left but can be a downfall in real estate. You can't be trying to get more without willing to give out something, it's like you're pushing people away and this might lead to missing some deals all because your pride took overall.

Making your needs a priority shouldn't be your main: try and learn more about their needs which can benefit and satisfy you both.

When it comes to negotiating, one of the tips I would give is that **patience is involve**. Don't say anything right away when the other part

CHAPTER 10: Negotiation Tips when Buying a House

makes an offer. Use your time wisely, time is money and most times money requires time.

Staying in touch: check back with the seller every few weeks to know if they are coming back, while waiting make use of your time to refine your strategy.

Make research be full of information: know your numbers, do your calculation correctly both in and out. If you don't know the calculation in and out, the seller will venture on your lack of knowledge which you may end up losing.

Think about negotiating as a work that is being paid for not as a money you're saving. Make use of the advantages you get from earning money while you're negotiating. The best way to increase the profit of your project is figuring out how to negotiate with the seller. You may feel like things are escalating when your agents negotiate. It can be stressful.

Increase your money deposit: it is the sum of money deposited to prove that you're serious about it. i.e., "earnest" (EMD) earnest money deposit.

Contingencies with care: a contingency can also be an incidental expense. Reducing the number of contingencies, you're requesting for, it's actually a way of saving. Some contingencies are too important to give up but try and be selective.

INVESTING IN REAL ESTATE: Flipping Houses

Home buyers are to pay their closing stocks for taxes, lender's fee and the title company fees. You can sell out between 4% or less of the home's sales price. The seller pays an additional 1% to the 4%.

A home warranty: Sometimes Sellers offer it to prospective buyers. It covers the cost of repairing home appliances and so on if they break down within a period of time.

Let's take an example: A home warranty cost $400 to $500 a year, if it's looking like waiving the home a warranty can improve negotiations, you might still want the peace of having one, just explain to the seller that they don't need to cover it, then you can buy it yourself.

Whether you're buying the warranty, or the seller is buying it, you will still need to pay the service fee between $50 and $100 and if something does, there would be a need to be repaired while under warranty.

There's strong correlation between the first offer and a final outcome. According to the anchoring principle, the first offer made in a negotiation sets us a powerful, unconscious psychological that acts as a gravitational force. So, if your first offer is too generous, you won't get a credit for it, avoid making an outrageous opening offer. Sometimes, most negotiators believe that they can establish by making an extreme offer, but it backfires and has an effect.

Ideally, be sure that your offer should be close to what you think about the other party best alternative to a negotiated offer. Also being close to what your buyer will pay or the least your seller would agree to.

CHAPTER 10: Negotiation Tips when Buying a House

Meanwhile, most people agree with a strong belief that they shouldn't come up with an opening offer. Most marketers can be so wise in the sense that they trick you into something cheaper than what it actually is. Let me make an example of a discount tag that has its original price on a pair of shoes, but since you focus on the deal, you're getting somewhat of what you're paying for.

Chapter 11

Financing

Before you can flip a house, you must own the property first. This is where you'll need good credit to qualify for one of the following types of real estate financing. However, if you don't have good credit now, don't worry: There are still some ways you can buy your first property and enter the flipping business.

CHAPTER 11: Loans vs. Other People's Money

1. Conventional Financing

A mortgage broker or a large banking institution does this. They base your ability to qualify for a loan on your current financial situation strictly (e.g., credit score, income, assets, debt). Without good credit, reasonable income, and a low amount of debt, you probably won't qualify for this type of financing, but don't feel bad since most people won't be eligible for it.

While lenders offer low-interest rates, low loan costs, and an extended loan duration for conventional financing, it's challenging to get because investors don't lend against properties that aren't move-in ready. For this reason, most lenders take a long time to appraise a house (usually 21 days), and if they're financing through Freddie Mac or Fannie Mae, which most do, you're limited to 4 – 10 loans at one time.

2. Portfolio/Investor Loans

Small banks (ones with only 3 – 5 branches) lend their own money; hence they're known as "portfolio lenders." They choose who they want to loan to, but your financial situation doesn't matter as long as you don't have a bankruptcy, foreclosure, or any large unpaid debts on your credit. They'll take your real estate experience and the type of deal you're seeking into consideration, though. With this said, if they feel you have a substantial investment, you'll likely receive financing.

Typically, you must put less than 30% down payment with these loans. Some of these will even offer you a "rehab loan," meaning they roll the rehab costs into your loan. In either case, they're mostly concerned in making sure you're about to make a sound investment. Since they're highly accustomed to doing this, they can usually close your loan in 7 – 10 days.

Most portfolio loans are short-term (6 – 12 months), so you must be confident, so you can finish the property and sell it in that amount of time. However, considering these loans usually have higher interest rates, it's in your best interest to complete the loan as soon as possible anyway. Also, remember the lender is very interested in your deal and will seriously scrutinize it. This is why they'll usually want to see that you have real estate experience.

3. Private Investors

These are well-off professionals (e.g., doctors, lawyers, business professionals) who have money (cash or retirement funds) to investors who expect better returns than what they'd receive from the stock market or other such venues, usually by about 8 - 12%. Often, you already know these people so you can approach them easily.

This is great if you can prove your ability to find and execute real estate deals; these investors typically don't care about your creditworthiness. However, it can take a lot of work to convince these people to trust you with their money because they usually don't have much experience with real estate. This is why you need a good business plan, a hard worker's track record, and trustworthiness.

4. Hard Money Lenders

A hard moneylender (a.k.a. HML) loans against the property's value instead of against you, the borrower. Typically, they pool funds from wealthy people then lend the money to you at a high rate. These are good loans for new investors with little cash or experience because you can get them quickly.

While these loans are available, regardless of your financial situation, there are some definite drawbacks. For instance, they'll often charge you a higher lending rate. It would be best to consider whether the money is worth the charges, but there are times when an HML will lend you 100% of both the purchase and rehab costs. However, considering the interest rates, which are usually 15% or more, this can eat up your profit margin rather quickly.

5. Equity Investors

These lenders will lend you money in return for a fixed percentage of the investment and the profit. They're more commonly known as a "partner with cash" because while you do all the work, you ultimately split the profit and only receive 50% of it as they take the other 50%. The beautiful thing is there are no "requirements" for you to fulfill so you can receive a loan since you're usually working with a friend or family member.

Besides the fact the lender takes 50% of your profit, another drawback to working with an equity investor is they typically want to take an active role in your investment. This is good only if they're experienced and share in your vision. Otherwise, it's usually a recipe for disaster.

Chapter 12

How to Choose the Right Loan for You

When you're ready to check on which of these investors is a good fit, prepare yourself to have the following five key components of your financial resume scrutinized:

INVESTING IN REAL ESTATE: Flipping Houses

Make sure you know your credit history and score. These numbers are important for getting your deals funded. You want a score of at least 680, or you'll find yourself immediately dismissed from consideration.

Assets such as cash in the bank, stocks, bonds, large retirement accounts, property ownership, and investment properties all make your lender feel more comfortable working. This is because these things are useful when it's time to collateralize against your loan. However, be aware that if you can't repay your loan, the lender gets your collateral.

Large amounts of debt make it difficult for you to get financing because lenders feel it will impede your ability to repay your loan. However, if you have a lot of debt (e.g., rent/mortgage, monthly bills, etc.) compared to your income, you have a better chance of getting a loan with a low-interest rate (ideally, under 30%).

Large amounts of debt make it difficult for you to get financing because lenders feel it will impede your ability to repay your loan. However, if you have a lot of debt (e.g., rent/mortgage, monthly bills, etc.) in comparison to your income, then you have a better chance of getting a loan with a low-interest rate (ideally, under 30%).

Investing experience is also of concern to some lenders because those with a long investment history are much less of a risk than inexperienced investors. If you're inexperienced, a good business plan is sometimes a good substitute as it shows you have a well thought out plan and clear direction.

CHAPTER 12: How to Choose the Right Loan for You

Flipping When You Have no Money

If you're like most aspiring investors today, you don't have any cash, credit, or money. This isn't something that should stop you, though. Instead, spend some time searching for another investor to partner with an HML or private lender.

When you do find someone willing to lend you money, you must know these tips for successful borrowing:

They'll look at your credit score to decide if you're creditworthy. This is why you shouldn't borrow too much money and always repay what you owe on time.

Make sure you understand the interest rate (the amount you're charged for borrowing the money) and the loan's terms. Look for things like statements saying they'll charge you a penalty rate for prepaying your mortgage, or there are late fees if your credit isn't paid by a certain time each month.

Think carefully about how much money you borrow. Since you're charged an interest rate, you'll ultimately end up paying back more money. This is why you don't want to borrow more money than you need or can afford.

The application process requires you to give your lender various types of information (e.g., credit score, proof of income). You'll want to know what information to take when you're applying for a loan, especially if you need the money immediately.

INVESTING IN REAL ESTATE: Flipping Houses

Know what the repayment period (how long you have to repay your loan) is. The shorter the repayment period, the less interest you'll pay, but this also requires you to pay slightly more on your loan.

Have a plan for repaying the loan before borrowing the money.

Chapter 13
Leverage or Not?

Real estate investing gets more exciting and potentially more rewarding when you make money with other peoples' money. That's where learning about investment property financing and real estate leverage comes in handy.

Leverage in real estate simply means how much money you borrow to finance an investment property compared to the property's worth. We use the term "leverage" because we're leveraging other people's money to maximize our ability to buy more investment properties with less of your own money. The higher your leverage, the higher your potential ROI (Return of Investment).

Leveraging money to make your purchase is key. Leveraged real estate investing can increase the profit margin on your investment properties. For example, let's say you have $50,000 cash on hand. You can use that money to do 3 things:

- Buy a $50,000 investment property with all the cash you have on hand. This equals a 0% leverage.
- Buy a $100,000 investment property with the $50,000 cash you have on hand and use an investment property financing method – like a bank mortgage loan – to borrow $50,000. This equals a 50% leverage.
- Buy a $200,000 rental property using the $50,000 cash you have on hand and use an investent property financing method to borrow $150,000.
- Buy two properties with $100k with $25k down in each property, 75% leverage on down payment.

We often are searching for where we will find the funds to get our investments started. Well there are several ways. Borrowing from your 401k, using a HELOC (home equity line of credit), personal loan, private money, hardmoney or from saved money. Your 401K or a HELOC is the cheapest and suggested ways. Be prepared for the repayment and payment schedule on both.

CHAPTER 13: Leverage or Not?

To calculate leverage for your rental property, simply divide your investment property fiancinng amount by the property value. This is also known as the loan-to-value ratio.

Leveraged real estate investing works best when rents and property values are rising. As rents and the value of the real estate investment rise, their monthly mortgage for rental property remains constant, creating larger and larger profits. Today's rents and property values are appreciating handsomely. This is the ideal environment for the real estate investor who knows how to leverage real estate investments with borrowed money.

Contemplate on our investment strategies. Many investors build their portfolio with rental properties in locations of low appreciaition but high net operating income (NOI).

Net operating income (NOI) is a calculation used to analyze the profitability of real estate investments that generate income. Net operating income equals all revenue from the property minus all reasonably necessary operating expenses.

While other investors look to build their portfolios in locating where the NOI amny be equal or lower, the area has a typical higher rate of appreciation on the assest/property.

A good rate of appreciation of 3-5% per year. These are considered loacations with high rates of appreciation. Some locations do not appreciate at all or very little over the long time spans of 10 years, for example.

Overall, you shouldn't fail to review your finances, stability and overall financial activity at least once a week. Financing is a tool to accomplish your goals. Try to avoid getting worked up over the minute details of the loan. Find a property that fits your goals, and a loan that allows you to accomplish those goals, and be happy.

Remember that other options like assumable financing, land sale contracts, and hard-money lending are all available to complete the deal, and that is what you want.

Chapter 14

Loans vs. Other People's Money

1. Banks

Do not be afraid! Banks can be a great tool if you know what banks to use and why to use them.

When looking for a Bank to do business with, you need to assess all they offer for a small business. Big banks do not always give small businesses breaks in account balances or discounts on wire fees, so you need to look around.

Credit unions are typically more comfortable to work with regard to flexible terms for independent business owners and small businesses. Even better is a small hometown credit union that typically has three branches or less. They want the community business and offer incentives for new accounts, business owners, and the small business itself.

As you converse with the Bank, you may add or remove questions or expand on them. As long as they will meet your needs as an investor, that is what is most important.

Use your bank incentives and get to know the tellers and branch managers. This will help you build rapport for future needs, such as borrowing. It also lends to other potential opportunities, such as referrals to other bank customers looking to invest. If the Bank has to foreclose on a property, they may call and offer it to you and with every relationship. There comes a time where you may get approved for something because of your relationship at that particular branch that you may not have had the opportunity for at a different location where the person does not know you.

2. Borrowing

Borrowing funds for investing is a standard part of the industry. Paying cash is ideal, but lending against or refinancing the investment to get the cashback keeps the wheel rolling. Let's look at a few borrowing scenarios:

- **Private Lending** is borrowing funds from a private individual or entity for an agreed-upon return. This can be based on a personal relationship, the asset, or a combination of both. Also, this may or may not be recorded against the investment and is determined between you and the lender.

    Private lending is lent with an interest amount in addition to the funds lent. If you borrow $100,000.00 at 10% interest, you will pay back $110,000.00 to the lender. The terms of this type of borrowing can be varied for the deal and amount of money lent. Private money can be lent for 30 days, 90 days, or a year whatever the parties agree to. You can make monthly interest payments and a balloon payment back at the end of the term, you can make monthly payments for the entire balance, or you can make one lump sum payment at the end of the term - for example, when the investment is flipped and sold.

- **Hard Money Lending:** One of the most common forms of borrowing for newer investors because it is easier to get and is generally based on the asset you are borrowing against. Hard money requires "points plus interest." Points are meaning a percentage of the loan amount PLUS the agreed-upon interest rate. For example, on a $100,000.00 hard money loan, you may have 2 points and 10%. Meaning you will pay $2,000.00 plus $10,000.00 in interest. Terms again agreed upon by the parties, but the option to pay it all at the end is removed. Hard money is lent for the term of the project. If you are flipping, the loan must be paid back upon selling or refinancing the investment. The points charged in a hard money loan are paid upfront at the beginning of the loan and monthly interest payments with a balloon at the end of the term. Hard money loans are often recorded as a lien against the investment as well.

- **Bank Lending:** Traditional lending with a bank is more detailed and requires personal and business records to validate the ability to pay back the loan. You will need to provide tax returns, pay stubs, profit, and loss statements for other investments and often carries a personal guarantee along with a business backing of the loan. The Bank will look at your credit score and history.

  Bank lending has an annual percentage rate charged against the loan amount and is paid monthly. Bank lending is a longer-term with lower interest rates and is recorded against the investment. So, on a $100,000.00 loan, you may pay 6% interest annually over 15 years, and you make a monthly payment until the loan is paid off.

3. Refinancing

Once you purchase an investment property and decide to keep it as a rental, you can refinance it and pull out most of the money put in with a manageable mortgage that the tenant would cover through their monthly rental amount plus give you a small profit. This is called a cash-out refinance. Many banks will offer this type of lending, but the banks you

CHAPTER 14: Loans vs. Other People's Money

want to use are the portfolio lending institutions. Frequently, they will lend up 80% of the appraised value, which should pull out all the funds you have in plus a little so you can move on to the next deal.

One of the great things here is that once you build a basic refinance relationship, you can expand into a purchase and rehab lending scenario with this same lender to buy and renovate properties which they can roll over from a rehab loan to a general loan once it's rented and generating cash flow.

4. Retirement Funds

Using retirement funds are a great way to build your retirement virtually tax-free. Using your IRA, you can borrow funds, buy an investment, and go back into your IRA account tax-free. Depending on the type of IRA you have, you may have to pay taxes to borrow upfront, but on a self-directed IRA, that money is paid when you transfer money out of a traditional IRA to the Self- Directed IRA. Then you can borrow without any further penalty. But again, app proceeds must go back into the IRA.

You can use someone else's retirement funds as well to do deals. This is a great way to borrow money but paying back the IRA your initial investment and any interest agreed to at the end of the investment term. IRA holders love to make money tax-free and will often lend purchase price and rehab amounts for the investment as long as they get all their funds plus interest back. So, you are flipping an investment, making a profit, and using none of your own money.

INVESTING IN REAL ESTATE: Flipping Houses

There are several other very creative ways to borrow funds, and each one can be as unique as the project you are using it on. Feel free to be creative with avenues, and don't be afraid to think outside the box when using funds to do a deal. Just make sure you read the contracts, understand what is expected of you in return for using the money, and what the terms are for repayment.

5. Home Equity Line of Credit or HELOC

A HELOC is a form of lending that allows you to borrow against the equity you already have in a property. This type of borrowing requires you to submit personal documents to the banks and have the property appraised to evaluate how much you can borrow. For example, if you own a house-personal or investment - that appraises $200,000.00, and you have a loan or mortgage on it for $110,000.00, there is $90,000.00 in equity.

Each lending institution offers a different percentage of the open equity for a loan, so you will need to ask that question. So out of $90,000.00 in equity, you may get $75,000.00 - it is up to the lender's terms. That being said, $75,000.00 is a great lump of cash to use for purchase, rehab, or partnership. Each month, you make a payment on the HELOC, which lowers the amount out on loan, so each month, your payments may be less and less since you have less equity pulled out on the property.

A HELOC can be used on anything really, but if you decide to go forward with a HELOC, then use the funds for something that will

CHAPTER 14: Loans vs. Other People's Money

benefit your retirement or cash flow long term.

6. Line of Credit

The standard line of credit comes in 2 forms - Secured and Unsecured.

A Secured line of credit is a loan you get approved for, and the lender uses something as collateral against the funds borrowed. Collateral depends on how much you want to borrow. That way, if you default on the loan, the Bank can seize the asset for repayment.

An Unsecured Line of Credit is where the Bank feels you hold enough merit based on your financials to repay the loan, and you are personally guaranteeing you will pay it back. Your signature is golden and means that you promise to pay the loan back no matter what.

7. No Money Investing

Nothing is saying you need to be wealthy to invest in real estate. There are no rules about where to get the funds to buy or renovate properties, and nothing is saying that you need to do any deal as a private business entity. Consider partnering with other investors who have the capital to spend but do not have the time or know-how to buy or renovate. Joint ventures and partnerships are a great alternative for both sides.

If you don't have money to buy a flip property, make use of your (OPM) other people's money to buy the property and the project expenses. Other people's money like, business partners, friends or family that have money to fund your project. With absolutely no money for flipping houses, you will need to create financial opinion to use little or no money for flipping houses.

You can partner with someone who can provide funds to find the deal when you don't have money to flip or you don't want to take debt. To partner with the person, you need to bring something to the table, I mean providing at least some cash to fund. Another mindset is working as an employee for a local house flipper. Go for real estate association, attend their meetings and network with other investors in your area, you can talk to them.

Many individuals are cash-rich but have no knowledge or time to do the research needed to purchase an investment, do not have the time to coordinate contractors or manage a renovation on investment, and they regularly look for individuals who have the knowledge and time to do just that and are willing to give up a portion of the cash flow for that time and effort. Part of the cash flow is better than no cash flow at all.

Partnering requires a more mature level of communication and confidence that you know what you are doing and that you can indeed offer something to them of value. These individuals often scrutinize things a little closer than the average investor. They prefer to know as many facts as they can and analyze the information before making the decisions to move forward. Once they gather the information needed, they will expect a contract or written agreement to line out the partnership's details and how the cash flow will flow in and how it will be divided between the parties.

CHAPTER 14: Loans vs. Other People's Money

You can have a joint venture agreement or partnership agreement drafted by a local attorney or use one that another investor doing partnerships may be using. It is important to ensure that both parties agree to the terms and sign the agreement before the transaction ensues. Once the investment comes through, and cash flow is generated, a good accounting system needs to be used so that at any time, an accurate account of the finances can be shared and viewed by all parties. In the end, investment funds are disseminated according to the agreement, and parties go their respective ways.

Using other people's money also works in ways, and you learned you could use funds from other sources to buy, renovate, and generate cash flow in many ways.

All of this can work for the good of all parties. In cases where the projects may not go as planned, or a deal goes over budget, there can be challenges that need to be considered. When other people funds are used, those funds must be replaced before anyone even considers making a profit. You want to ensure that those with the funds are made as whole as possible, so even if the profit is much less or non-existent, their initial investment is returned to them. This is the most ethical way to ensure that your reputation and ability to do right by your funding sources are foremost in the contractual agreement.

Another strategy called wholesaling, which means getting a property at a discount and re-assigning the contract for another buyer. With this means of flipping, you would not need funds for the property.

INVESTING IN REAL ESTATE: Flipping Houses

Chapter 15

Home Renovation

The greater part of the work associated with a fixer-upper real estate investment is identified with the home renovation process. While home-renovation isn't a procedure that is selective to investment properties, and numerous homebuyers buy homes that needs renovation with the expectation of moving into the house subsequent to redesigning it, the way toward making arrangements for home renovation for a fixer-upper investment is totally different from home renovation for proprietor occupiers.

When getting ready for a home renovation, a real estate investor needs to remember that the primary motivation behind revamping the real estate property is to make a benefit from selling it. Normally, any real estate investor who is thinking about a fixer-upper needs to remember that the higher the home renovation costs are, the less benefit they will make when selling the property. Be that as it may, simultaneously, a real estate investor will need to apply enough renovation takes a shot at the property to successfully expand its fairly estimated worth so as to make a higher benefit. Along these lines, so as to discover the equalization

INVESTING IN REAL ESTATE: Flipping Houses

when arranging the costs versus included an incentive for your investment, you as a real estate investor would need to accumulate a decent measure of data and information on home renovation, its expenses, and its sorts so as to have the option to accomplish their objectives.

CHAPTER 15: Home Renovation

Renovating an old home restores value because it makes the property livable and aesthetically appealing. After all - no one could ever see themselves living in a run-down shack! Buyers gravitate towards fresh coats of paint and clean new tiles, so it's essential to make those changes if you want to reel in buyers without pushing such a hard sell.

Just like the home selection process, there are a few guidelines you should keep in mind when planning a renovation. These key points should help direct you towards making the right choices, so you get the best returns out of your effort without having to spend more than you're willing to or capable of.

The Foundations of a Cost-Effective Renovation

Flipping a home is sinking a lot of thousand dollars in a renovation, even if you really want to do the work yourself and you've created time for it, the materials and supplies would cost a lot of money. Ensure you know your prices for materials as well as what a job would cost on the total project budget.

Understanding what's necessary and what luxury is sets the boundaries and helps keep your budget in order. As a general rule, you'll want to do the least without sacrificing build quality and aesthetics. This will help maintain your project within reasonable cost and time limits without affecting its appeal to your prospective buyers.

Do better work but focus more on paying for better quality work and things that will make the finished product better. You don't have to overspend but you should understand the design.

Keep in Line with Competition

You probably thought that the first step to planning a renovation is doing

CHAPTER 15: Home Renovation

a thorough inspection of your property. But on the contrary, the first step is scoping other similar properties for sale in your area. Sound funny? It does, but there's an entirely valid explanation.

If your home looks worse, buyers might be more inclined to purchase slightly more expensive houses to avoid making any changes on their own. If your home is too renovated, you might have spent too much to get your property to look way different while weighing its cost. Sure, it seems banging' - but with a far smaller budget, prospective purchasers can get decent features in the same area that are just as livable.

Essentially, what you want is to look even just slightly better than the competition. You don't need to pay for such expensive changes that make you exceptionally different - all you need to aim for is cleaner and fresher! In many cases, that could mean just allowing a few cosmetic changes to give your house that brand-new look and feel.

Know When to DIY

We're not all home improvement experts, so you will need to hire a contractor somewhere down the line… but do you? Perhaps during your own homeownership experience, you've had to oversee a few home improvement projects.

These likely ranged from simple repainting jobs to woodworking and everything in between. Whatever the case, it was cheaper to get it done by yourself and a few subcontractors instead of hiring a general contractor to do the job.

INVESTING IN REAL ESTATE: Flipping Houses

Unfortunately, the decision to push through as a DIY contractor might change if the house, you're dealing with is going to be sold for a profit. But then again, getting it done DIY means you can cut back on the cost and increase your net profit. So, what do you do?

There are a few things you can ask yourself if you want to find out whether you're ready to take on the job of a DIY contractor. Understanding where you stand in terms of these factors will give you a realistic idea regarding your readiness and capability to oversee the operations yourself.

- Do you have the time and availability to be present on-site throughout the renovation process?
- Are you comfortable working with your hands and getting things done using power tools, construction materials, etc.?
- Are the repairs and renovations required within your set of skills?
- Do you have contacts with subcontractors to do more tedious, technical jobs for you?
- Do you possess some knowledge of home improvement and renovation?
- Are you confident in your capability to generate outcomes comparable to a professional contractor given the tasks you intend to do yourself?

If you answered no to any of these questions, you might be better off seeking a pro. Look - we're not underestimating your capabilities, and,

CHAPTER 15: Home Renovation

indeed, everyone can learn to get home improvements done DIY-style. But taking a gamble with investment could mean more expenses down the line.

If you end up ruining any part of the repairs, you might have to call in a pro anyway and end up making extra payments for more renovations than you initially required.

Even if you manage to get the repairs done all by yourself, there's quality. Does it look like something a potential buyer would be happy to see and pay for? Or will it likely deter prospective purchasers? If it doesn't improve your property's salability, you'd have to get a contractor anyway to clean things up for you.

Don't let the allure of saving 10% - 30% on renovation costs get the best of you - you should know what's best for your property! If you feel that you're biting off more than you can chew, you probably are.

Start with Bare Minimum

Remember - you're not aiming to create the next Better Homes and Gardens featured property. So, don't go overboard with the changes you want to make.

Generally, if you followed the right steps in the home selection process, the layout of your home should be suitable enough to work off without changing anything about the blueprint - which leads us to a guiding mantra in the process of fixing a flip.

INVESTING IN REAL ESTATE: Flipping Houses

Focus on the Cosmetic

Nicked paint, yellowish grout, broken tiles, leaky ceilings, old bathroom fixtures, creaky cabinet and cupboard doors, and other features that might make the home look unappealing should be the focus of your efforts. These don't make any changes to the property's overall footprint and are generally cheaper to get done.

If you got your home from an auction and weren't able to give it a closer inspection before sealing the deal, you might find a few structural damages when you finally get to walk inside.

Issues concerning windows, weight-bearing beams, rotten walls, damaged roofing, and other features of the home that have something to do with the framework of the house can be a setback in terms of both time and cost. It's also worth mentioning that these repairs typically require different permits before they can be started. So that adds to the expense on top of lengthening your timeline.

Again, it's worth reiterating that the house you choose will be pivotal to your project's profitability. Make the wrong choice at the start, and you might find yourself scrambling to figure out whether you can make a profit at all.

The 4 Kinds of Home Renovations

There are four different kinds of renovations that you can execute on

CHAPTER 15: Home Renovation

your property, and each of these increases the value and salability of your investment. Understanding which ones you need will help you develop a plan that maximizes your property's AFV without having to spend too much of your budget.

1. The Basics

Necessary renovations are changes and repairs that address features that buyers expect should be in good order. Ceilings that don't drip and leak in the rain, functional gutters and downspouts, a working furnace, and other essential aspects should be in good working condition if you want to attract buyers.

You don't necessarily have to renovate them all to the highest of standards - simple maintenance tasks and a few minor changes to get everything working can be more than enough.

Now the question - does basic renovation add value to your property? Not exactly. Buyers expect that houses for sale should have all of these basics to be considered viable options. Essentially, making sure that all of your investment's necessary features are operational simply brings your home up to standards.

So, should you get them done? Absolutely. If your home doesn't have all of these basic adequately addressed, you might not be able to reel in any buyers in the first place.

2. Curb Appeal

These renovations improve the aesthetic appeal of your property. Again, they don't necessarily add value, but they will help make your house sell faster. Investing in these changes can make your property look handsome and inviting from the moment buyers take a glance, making it easier for them to visualize their life there and hopefully develop an attachment that drives profitable action.

Renovations that improve curb appeal include a well-manicured lawn, fresh coats of exterior and interior paint, clean carpets, and other cosmetic changes that make the place look neat and appealing.

Keep in mind though that some curb appeal changes might only really appeal to you. So instead of trying to flex your interior design muscle, try to keep it simple. Neutral paint colors, a tasteful backsplash, and dull, clean bathroom tiles with white grout can be better than trying to impress buyers with your taste in unconventional bohemian inspired design.

3. Value-Adding

Now we move on to the aspect of renovation that improves the ARV of your investment. These changes focus on the house features that make it easier or more convenient to live in.

For instance, houses with updated HVAC systems that are eco-friendly and energy-efficient are likely to save their homeowner the added expense of clunky, outdated systems. The same goes for ranges and range hoods that are more efficient at saving electricity and eliminating

CHAPTER 15: Home Renovation

foul odors from the interior space.

Value-adding renovations can be expensive at the get-go, so as a beginner, you might think they're not necessary. But because these changes can recoup up to 80% of their value once resale comes around, they can be incredibly beneficial for your endeavor.

Remember to stay within limits, though. Even if these changes add value, you don't want to be too different from the other houses in your vicinity. If you have state-of-the-art everything and the houses around just scream plain vanilla, your home might stick out… in the wrong way.

4. Preferential

This house would look so much better with a game room in place of that third bedroom! Before you okay the renovation, ask yourself - is this something you prefer, or is it a change that would get the thumbs up from anyone?

One major pitfall that many beginners succumb to when flipping their first house is treating it like home. The last thing you'd want is to make the mistake of developing an attachment to your investment, which might push you to make decisions that appeal more to your sense of "practicality" and "improvement" instead of the market's concept of the ideal.

The best way to stay grounded when planning out those changes is by checking out the competition. If most of the houses for sale in the area have three bedrooms and no game rooms, you'd be better off the following suit.

Other changes that fit into this category include hot tubs, wine cellars, swimming pools, and ponds. Not everyone wants them, and some might be a maintenance nightmare, making them a downside for practical buyers who want a home that's not hard to live in or to keep in good condition.

Chapter 16

Renovation Goals

The two key factors in esteeming private real estate are location and area. This is essential to recollect when making sense of what enhancements to include.

It is anything but difficult to over improve a property and end up with an item that is lovely yet overrated for its area. While a few purchasers may spend a limited quantity more for a progressively improved property, they won't almost certainly spend a critical sum more if there is nothing in the region selling at that high of a cost.

INVESTING IN REAL ESTATE: Flipping Houses

Keep in mind, not all upgrades include esteem. Such things as home workplaces, solid yards and sports courts by and large don't increase the value of a property. Be mindful so as not to spend your cash on things that will confine the quantity of individuals keen on the property.

Take a gander at houses that are available in the zone. Which ones are selling the quickest? What enhancements do they share practically speaking? Presently take a gander at the ones that have sat available the longest. What do they share practically speaking? Take in an exercise from both of these sorts of properties to decide how to boost your arrival on home enhancements.

1. Build up a Strong First Impression

Have you ever a sat in front of the TV real estate appear, similar to "House Hunters" on HGTV or "Million Dollar Listing" on Bravo? The one thing that these shows share for all intents and purpose is that when they are demonstrating a house, they quite often show the potential purchaser's early introduction while showing up at the property.

It is likewise certain that regardless of what is happening inside a house, a negative early introduction upon appearance is difficult to return from. The exercise is to ensure that your property has incredible check advance, with the goal that the potential purchaser anticipates seeing what is inside.

To begin with, you have to ensure that the structure itself is as pleasant as it very well may be. Force wash the siding, naturally paint all trim

CHAPTER 16: Renovation Goals

work, ensure that window housings are in acceptable condition, and so forth. Doing simple restorative fixes can have a major effect.

A few recommendations for things that will give you a huge explosion for your buck include:

- Sprucing up the front entryway by painting it a differentiating shading
- Supplanting old outside equipment like door handles
- Making the portal balanced
- Introducing open air lighting
- Planting blossoms and plants
- Introducing another letter box
- Including shades

A large portion of these are not over the top expensive, yet alongside your showcasing plan they will have an immense effect in pulling in the correct purchaser at the best cost.

2. Kitchens and Bathrooms Sell the House

In the profoundly serious private home deals showcase, you can't have a dated kitchen or bathroom and hope to get as much as possible for your property. Not exclusively are these enhancements the way to getting a decent cost for your home flip, yet they are urgent for getting individuals intrigued. They will unquestionably diminish the days a property spends available.

INVESTING IN REAL ESTATE: Flipping Houses

As per US News, the normal kitchen redesign in the United States runs $16,000 and the normal expense of a bathroom makeover is $10,000. These are probably the best renovations for resale as they will make buyers begin to look all starry eyed at your property and pay for themselves.

Few out of every odd kitchen and bathroom needs a total redesign, yet practically all require some refreshing. Dispassionately take a gander at the current kitchen cupboards. Do they should be supplanted, or would they be able to be restored, refaced or painted?

Simply recollect, while improving a kitchen, it is critical to make it safe and family agreeable. For instance, ensure that every single electrical outlet is appropriately grounded and are the necessary good ways from water sources. Ensure the floor is slip safe and that counters have adjusted edges.

With respect to bathrooms, it might be conceivable that the current tile can be utilized, and the apparatuses, for example, toilets and sinks supplanted. Refreshing a shower entryway, or equipment in the room might be a simple fix. Like a kitchen, any work done must protect that the room is sheltered.

Remodeling a dated kitchen can build your odds to get as much as possible for your property.

3. Try not to Impose Your Personal Style

CHAPTER 16: Renovation Goals

Concentrating on impartial structure components will speak to the biggest purchasing crowd.

Nothing turns purchasers off more than awful taste. Obviously, what is awful taste is subjective depending on each person's preferences? Be exceptionally cautious on forcing what you accept is your outrageous acceptable taste on a property.

For instance, you may feel that brilliant green rock is a delightful material for your kitchen counters, yet the vast majority won't concur with you. First-class things, similar to ledges, bathroom installations, covering and divider completions ought to be in hues that intrigue to the best number of clients.

As needs be, delicate, unbiased hues ought to quite often be utilized. There is space to utilize brilliant hues and surprising materials as accents to cause to notice things, yet they ought to never be prevail. They ought to consistently be contacts, not overpowering sums.

4. Cost

Try not to invest more into the property than what the property is worth.

Flippers as often as possible get so enveloped with ventures that they stray from their strategy and radically overspend on a property. At the point when this occurs, they are totally stunned when they don't make a benefit on their flip.

It is anything but difficult to forget about expenses and over improve a property, in a craving to convey a specific wow factor. While you do need that wow factor, you should be cautious about how to accomplish it.

Before beginning a house flip, ensure you distinguish where you will go through a great deal of cash and where you are most certainly not. While there might be cost invades, that is the thing that the possibility support is for. In the event that you wind up overspending your recovery spending plan and possibility finance, you will wind up losing cash on your home flip.

Contractual worker costs should likewise be firmly checked. While numerous temporary workers are straightforward, not every one of them are. Contractual workers every now and again overbuy materials, for example, sheetrock, plumbing things, tile, and so forth and get paid for the materials by the rehabber. The contractual worker may then restore a portion of the overbought things to the store where bought and keep the cash.

In different cases, a contractual worker may have a dumpster put at a rehabber's home, however, permit others that he is partnered with to utilize it. The rehabber is then stuck paying extra for the expanded weight. Trust your contractual worker, yet in addition, watch out for the primary concern. Keep in mind - the ultimate objective is to sell, so center around the best renovations for resale.

Home renovation is, with no uncertainty, the most significant part of

CHAPTER 16: Renovation Goals

any fixer-upper or fix-and-flip real estate investment.

In case you're keen on a fixer-upper sort investment in the real estate advertise, at that point it is critical for you to have a total comprehension of the various parts of home renovation, its sorts, its expenses, and how to discover the harmony between all the various factors so as to accomplish an effective real estate investment.

Thus, with no further ado, we should begin.

Chapter 17

Tips to Increase Home Value

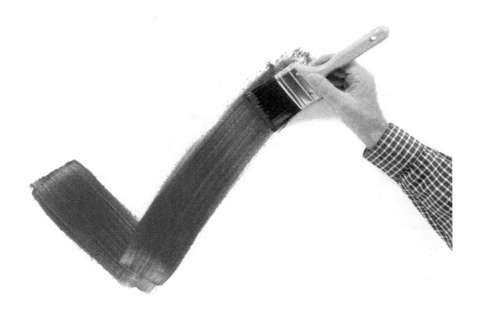

For many real estate investors, determining what it is likely to cost to renovate a given property is often enough to swing a potential investment in one way or another. While it can be hard for new real estate investors to determine just how much everything is going to cost, here are some tips to ensure you can manage any renovation for as little out of pocket as possible. Here are overall renovation tips:

CHAPTER 17: Tips to Increase Home Value

1. Start by Breaking Every Required Task Down as Much as Possible

While it can be stressful to think of everything that needs to be done to get a property show-ready, especially if you picked it up cheap because it needed a lot of work, you will find that it is helpful to break every task down into its primary components. This makes it easier for you to determine what projects you or your friends and family can take care of without professional help, but it will help make all of those tasks seem more manageable. You will want to go room by room and make a list of everything that needs to be changed before you can rent it out.

If you are planning on doing as much of the project yourself as possible, and it is your first time tackling this sort of thing, then your best bet is to start in the laundry room, where available typically. The reasons for this are two-fold, first, the place generally is on the small side, and there likely won't be all that much that needs to be done with space outside of cleaning and maybe a new coat of paint which means you can use a small success to bolster your confidence moving forward. Even better, if things don't exactly break your way, you have only messed up one of the least important rooms in the house instead of something high like the bathroom or the kitchen.

2. Keep Costs in Check

Keep in mind, renters are not buyers, so everything does not need to be perfect, which means that you can realistically expect to skimp in some areas that would otherwise need to be dealt with if you were trying to sell the property in question. When deciding what to renovate, a good rule of thumb is only to make changes that you can expect to double your investment on. That means that you need to know how you are going to get two dollars back for every dollar you spend.

Depending on the property in question, one great place to go to make a quick profit is outside were repainting the exterior and redoing any cement rendering can generally be expected to bring in as much as 10 dollars per dollar invested. Another area where you will likely see big returns is if you spruce up the front and backyard, where applicable, and maybe even put in a garden. The return here is generally five dollars for every dollar spent, though this can increase depending on the quality of your results.

3. Don't Overestimate the Little Things

While they can easily add significant value to a property, many new real estate investors focus on the bigger issues that need to be taken care of that they often let the little things repair. Little things like old outlet covers, dirty fans, old fixtures, chipped doorframes all add up to your detriment, however, which means you are going to want to ensure these things are gone over specifically before you start showing the property. The best exterior and most modern of kitchens can't make up for numerous little signs that a property has seen better days. Give all of your major improvements a chance to shine by ensuring potential renters have nothing else to look at.

CHAPTER 17: Tips to Increase Home Value

When it comes to making minor improvements, including interior painting, it can be natural for new real estate investors to try and save a few dollars here and there by purchasing the cheapest products to fill the need in question as possible. This is likely to cost you more in the long run, however, as cheap products are typically cheap or a reason. Do yourself a favor in the long run and prioritize quality in all of your projects.

4. Seek Out Smaller Suppliers

While running to the closest big box home improvement store is often the quickest and easiest choice, it is rarely going to be the cheapest, especially if you take the time to shop around beforehand. While you might have to go to different places for different items instead of getting everything in one fell swoop, you can save as much as 25 percent by striking a deal with a local owner.

When you go in to discuss your needs with the owner of a store, it is important to express yourself and your purpose clearly, while at the same time also making it very clear that you are planning on doing a lot of this type of business moving forward and that you are just checking around regarding bulk prices.

When going about this process, it is important never to take the first offer that you are given and to instead find multiple prices to get owners to one-up each other in the process. While making these deals, it is important not to go in dressed to the nines in your most expensive

INVESTING IN REAL ESTATE: Flipping Houses

clothes and accessories as this will naturally cause many people to try and charge you more for the same services as a result.

5. Make Repairs a Party

While there are likely going to be many little things that need doing around your property, just because you are avoiding using your contractor as much as possible doesn't mean you have to do everything yourself. Numerous little jobs need doing, no experience required, which means that if you get a group of friends together and make a day of it, you can take care of lots of the small stuff in a single day. Unpaid labor is great for lots of things, including laying tile, cleaning or removing baseboards, landscaping, fencing, painting, replacing outlet covers, and more.

6. Always Be on the Lookout for Good Bargains

You never know where you are going to come across something that would be useful in a rental down the road which means that if you are always on the prowl, you can virtually guarantee you will find useful items for a steep discount if you avoid buying them at the moment when convenience is king. Especially when it comes to appliances, you will be surprised how much you can save on things like floor models, discontinued items, or those that are functional but have cosmetic damage (truly the best rental appliances).

One easy place to add value while still finding a good bargain is when it comes to the type of countertop used in the bathroom. Granite

CHAPTER 17: Tips to Increase Home Value

countertops add a touch of class to any space, and the fact that much of your space is going to be taken up by a sink in a bathroom can allow you to pick up otherwise expensive granite for a deeply discounted. To do so, all you need to do is look for flawed pieces of granite, the flawed the better than, as long as it is situated in the middle of the granite piece.

7. Consider the Long Term

While it can be easy to focus on the simplest solution for renovating properties for rental purposes, there are certain areas where going above and beyond will save you money in the long term without directly contributing to what you can charge for rent. Little things like LED lights or enhanced insulation will save your renter's money and save you money during the occasions when you have to pay for utility costs. Likewise, if you take the time to install a sprinkler system that is on a timer, then you won't need to worry about taking the time to redo the landscaping every time a renter moves out who couldn't be bothered to move a house around the yards regularly.

8. Go Green

There are also several types of renovations that you can consider that will not only be good for the environment but will also be good for your profit margin. These days, people are conscientious when it comes to the environment and, even better for you, will come into the situation trained to pay more for things that play into their eco-guilt. The most profitable of these types of renovations are currently solar panels, which, while expensive, will pay for themselves countless times over what you can charge in increased rent. In this scenario, you can easily add 80 percent of the average electric bill to each month's rent and still have people happy for the privilege.

9. Be Creative

When it comes to renovating on as tight of a budget as possible, it can help to focus on creative ways to work with what you have, instead of replacing everything right away at first blush. Instead of simply pulling out everything in the bathroom and the kitchen, consider what can be done in resurfacing cabinets or repainting fixtures, tubs, showers, and tiles. While the specifics of what you are going to do will vary by home, with a little online research, you can likely come up with countless creative ways to spruce things up while still paying as little as possible.

The key here is to be willing to compromise on your overall vision in realistic ways without dramatically decreasing the result's overall quality. To determine what refurbishments are required, so you don't have to worry about deciding at the moment, you will want to make a list early on of the absolute requirements followed by those things that would be nice in a perfect world, as well as things that you might be able to do something about if the right solution came along at the right price. This will allow you to plan your budget accurately and stick to it in the heat of the moment when you might want to go another way for one reason or another.

Chapter 18
Tips for a Successful Closing

Pricing your home correctly shouldn't be a bad idea, because when you price your home correctly once it gets to the market, but if you overprice a home in making an attempt to get money it will only be left there on the market without any buyer. However, I would suggest that you will get more money by pricing the home correctly with a potential bidding war than you would be overpricing it. When you price correctly, you should receive offers within a few weeks to help you sell the home as fast as possible. So, price your home correctly.

1. Knowing what improvement to make. When flipping houses, it's important to know which improvements to make. There is a possibility that you will lose a sale due to under-improving a property and an increase in your cost due to over-improvement. Be sure that you are aware of the necessary renovations and repairs to make as well as the upcoming trends. Try to suggest the newest technology in heating, ventilation, air conditioning, plumbing, electrical, appliances, and other home improvements if you have the budget to increase the value of your house.

2. Avoiding doing something too big especially if you're a newbie to the fix and flip business. Start with a single-family home and a rehab that will cost $50,000 or less. Buying a large property with a huge renovation investment would be too costly and can be very risky at times, especially when you are just starting out. So, start out right to avoid spending twice on properties. Make the right improvement and fix what is necessary. Always have it in mind that this is a business and you are not renovating a house to make it look like your dream home. Some of the mistakes that real estate agents do is that they spend money on unnecessary improvement.

3. You should not do all of these things listed above alone, partner

CHAPTER 18: Tips for a Successful Closing

with a seller who can help you negotiate a very low price but offer to give them a reasonable piece of the pie upon resale. The seller would likely accept a low sales price and it is known that they will get a cut out from the profit of the sale.

4. House flipping is a form of active investment. Successful real estate investors are those who understand and are aware of the risk factors and know how to eliminate them effectively. It is better to understand the risks involved in venturing into the real estate market. You might have found a property you want to flip by now to secure financing to buy the house and make the necessary renovations.

Keeping your profit margin in mind, which is important, so you'll want to do some research on providers before you take out a loan. It's best to get in touch with a reputable lender, so ask people and ask the agent who can refer you to a lender that doesn't charge much when paying back.

Know who is going to buy the property from you and knowing their price point to know if they are on the lower end price point of buyers in the area or the higher end? Also, you should only spend money in the effort of creating a product that you know someone in that market would buy.

5. The main goal of the flip is to sell it fast and make a profit. You should carefully and precisely calculate what your profit margin would be on any flip and weigh that against your costs, including your holding costs.

INVESTING IN REAL ESTATE: Flipping Houses

Making an impulsive purchase or buying the property "sight unseen" puts you at serious risk. so, an inspection is necessary to assess and know the condition of the property properly and make a budget for the repairs. It will help you create a detailed and accurate budget plan before applying for financing and also give you a clear understanding of how much funds you will need to complete the project successfully and sold for a profit.

When you're buying a house to fix and flip, focus on properties that need mostly cosmetic improvements. A home that needs a new roof or has an outdated electrical system will likely require too much money into the house to turn a healthy profit, so you should avoid homes with foundation problems unless you can fix it yourself. Focus on homes where lower-cost improvements can have a big impact like painting, new carpeting, refinishing hardwood floors, replacing trim and kitchen appliances. This would cost you a lot of money, and when you get home will fewer furnishings you would flip for a profit with not much cost.

6. Knowing the market and being in the right market. Choosing the wrong market will kill you on your very first deal. Knowing the market helps you in two ways I.e. doing the right type of upgrades that the market is ready to pay, and more importantly, there is a high likelihood and a buyer waiting to buy your finished product. So do your homework and farm an area where you want to flip. Since you will have to make several trips every day, having it closer to your house is the key.

7. You should also select the price range that is ideal for flipping. When it comes to flipping houses, investors with little flipping

CHAPTER 18: Tips for a Successful Closing

experience looking for hard money lenders would need to obtain large amounts of cash. Generally, this amount ranges from 25% to 50% of the sale (the down payment). However, investors can reduce this amount by negotiating a deal where the lender gets a percentage of the profit.

Some investors have a lot of experience and good track records, hard money lenders are more likely to assist with little to no private money or down payment from the borrowing party. Nonetheless, if some investors are new and low on money, there would be needed to ask around with the people they know, such as family and friends, with a promise of paying their money back and some of the profit.

Another good option is to find a wealthy business partner who will pay while you do the work because you need money to not only buy a home but also to rehab it to bring it up to sellable standards.

It can be difficult to get funding for a fix and flip. Traditional lenders usually require exact credit and often the process is always long. So, the best thing is to find a lender who works with flippers and have an easy application process, require a small portion of the down payment, and have a quick turnabout time.

Work with experienced title company in your area, get information from them and they will help you navigate the process.

8. Talk to a professional real estate agent in your local market which is very important and ensure that you make a profitable flip. Don't hesitate to ask your real estate agent a lot of questions about selling the property, they will help you with detailed information as a newbies and also, underestimating your area's closing costs is a mistake you'd not want to make. If you are not planning on conceding closing costs, surveys, and repairs, it can eat a big chunk of your potential profit.

No matter how you draft out your budget and your expected expenses, there is a good chance that a problem might come up which will make an added cost to your project. You don't want such unexpected things to break your project. It's better to a sufficient buffer in the budget for contingency expenses, typically around 20% or more.

9. If you are a newbie flipper, it's best to surround yourself with experienced and expert real estate investors. Join your local real estate investing (REI) club and attend their meetings which will help you to get more information and updates about flipping houses successfully, join as many social media groups on the subject as you can. You can post questions and read through their prior posts to learn more about flipping. You'll learn a lot from the experience of the experts which would give you through.

10. It is important to be conservative with your budget. When flipping houses, you should have a drafted budget especially when you're a beginner. Always leave a little cover in your budget for unexpected things that might come up. When you start opening up walls or doing demo to the property, there are bound to be extra things that need to be fixed as well as the little things you originally forgot to put in your budget.

Outline your budget for better flipping. When you make sure you have some buffer room in your budget which are conservative with your numbers, you'll be on your way to making a nice profit.

11. Get your value right, then you can get a whole lot of other things wrong and still make money. However, the reverse is rarely true. If you get the value wrong, it doesn't matter what you do, you're likely going to lose money. So, don't make any mistake of overpaying too much on properties and when you start with calculating an accurate 'after repair value,' or the price you could sell the house for after you are done fixing it up, there will be difference between the deal price and the ARV must be large enough to cover up the expenses and also make a profit.

12. Holding on a bad deal would cost you a lot of money. If you buy a house and find yourself considerably in over your head, resell it and move on quickly, even if it means you're selling at a loss. Every experienced investor has had to do this during their hard times.

13. Be logical with your renovation. Doing the math is to figure out what you can spend on both the house and the renovation, to the last dollar it would cost and include how much risk you are ready to take.

Chapter 19
Price Home Correctly

Flipping your property for maximum money doesn't mean pricing it as high as the sky! This is one of the biggest mistakes many house flippers make, usually as attempts to recoup their investments when they go overboard on their repair and renovation budgets.

It's tempting to look at your renovation and when you love what you've done, factor in all the equity and overvalue the home. Remember, your

CHAPTER 19: Price Home Correctly

buyer didn't see it when you started and they are not aware of how much stress you've gone through so far, they didn't know the kitchen was so horrible and the basement stunk. But all they could see is the finished product only. You've done well.

The main purpose of flipping a house is to find a buyer who's willing to pay a maximum price for your hard work. Where "maximum money" means the highest reasonable price based on recent market transactions and current selling prices for similar properties within the same area. If comparable properties in your property's county have been sold for between $50,000 and $55,000, the latter is a reasonable basis for "maximum" money. It wouldn't make sense to sell your property for $65,000 even if you believe that what your mind can conceive, your body will achieve!

There are three important keys to consider if you want to maximize the selling price of the house you're flipping:

1. Let a licensed and experienced real estate agent sell it for you.
2. Price the property right.
3. Make sure it's in very good condition.

Home Staging

Home staging is a nutshell – the practice of presenting a home that's up for sale in the best possible light. It's done depending on the parties responsible for doing it, e.g., the owner, the real estate agent, or professional home stagers.

One of the most common ways homes for sale are home staged is by filling it up with furniture and appliances that maximize its aesthetics, space, and flow. Others do it, like on property flipping shows on HGTV, via an open-house event where agents can bring their prospective buyers to see the place, often spruced up by furniture and appliances that don't come with the package.

While real estate agents are well-versed in selling and closing home sales, they're not necessarily the best when it comes to presenting a home in its most aesthetic form. They may be knowledgeable about the things that can help make a home very marketable. Still, if the objective is to present a home in its full potential glory, professional home stagers are the people for the job.

As their title implies, professional home stagers are experts in preparing homes for resale for maximum positive impact on potential buyers. They maximize a home's design and flow by, among other things:

- Eliminating clutter.
- Populate the house with furniture that complements its design and color scheme to show potential buyers how good it looks when already filled with furniture and appliances.
- Helping out optimize the house's curb appeal.

How important are first impressions when it comes to your goal of selling your property investment for top money? Those in the real estate

CHAPTER 19: Price Home Correctly

marketing profession know that without an excellent first impression, selling a house is very low. Why?

Even as prospective buyers pull into a house's driveway, they already start to have opinions and expectations of how the home may look like inside based on its curb appeal – their first point of contact with the house. As such, most homebuyers' minds are made up within the first minute after stepping into a house's front door. While it doesn't mean poor first impressions immediately doom the sale, it does make it so much harder to close it later on during the showing or staging.

That's the value of home staging a home for resale. It helps create excellent first impressions with any potential buyers that walk through its doors such that the chances of closing the sale at the seller's desired price are maximized.

How do you find capable professional home stagers? It's not that different from looking for a right contractor, e.g. through personal referrals and recommendations of your agent/broker, contractor, friends, family members, or other property flippers; and Sites like Craigslist, Angieslist, and HomeAdvisor.

How much do professional home stagers charge? Well, it depends, so the best way is to ask your home stager candidates for an estimate. Most of the time, they'd be more than willing to a free and quick estimate for their services.

Just remember that an estimate, by nature, isn't exact or cast in stone. There's always the possibility that costs can be higher or lower than estimated. However, the most experienced home stagers can estimate costs with relatively high accuracy such that deviations from estimates are insignificant.

Get free estimates from several home stager candidates and crunch numbers based on those estimates. These may vary from one professional home stager to another in terms of amount and basis, i.e., hourly rate or per job or project. That's why you must clarify each professional home stager's basis for charging fees so you can make a fairly good estimate of how much you'll spend for their services and the impact on your house flipping profits.

You should also clarify what professional home stagers plan to bring inside the house you're selling and how much those would cost. This is so you can avoid curveballs on your bill with the professional stager, should you decide to get one to maximize the price at which you can flip the house.

So, how do you decide if you should home stage or not? One factor to consider is the current market practice for similar properties in the same area. If most of them are sold at excellent prices without having to stage them, chances are you don't need to home stage the house. But if home staging's the thing in that market, you may need to do it.

If you're not going to home stage the house, you still have to make sure that it'll look useful to your prospective buyers. Here are some things you can do to make the house as enticing as possible without the home

CHAPTER 19: Price Home Correctly

stage:

1. Engage the services of professional deep cleaners to ensure the house is immaculately clean.
2. Ensure that the front yard, if it has one, is well-kept, i.e., pulled weeds, tidy, and mowed the lawn.
3. Keep all window blinds and curtains open during prospects' visits.
4. Keep the air-conditioner or heater at pleasant temperatures.
5. Trim away tree branches, if any, from the walkway.
6. If it's snowing, make sure the walkway, sidewalk, and driveways are shoveled. If it's fall, ensure the leaves are swept away from walkways, sidewalks, and driveways.

The Price is Right

The very first thing that your house's potential buyers will evaluate is its selling price. Both real estate agents and homebuyers usually sort their property searches on the MLS according to price, i.e., from the cheapest to the most expensive.

Many interested home buyers want to move into specific neighborhoods within a particular budget. This is where being aware of the average, maximum, and minimum selling prices of similar properties becomes necessary. If you don't know these numbers, you can price your house too much that no one will buy it or too low that the return on your investment may be too low. Also, pricing your property beyond the average range in the area will keep prospective buyers from even considering the house you're flipping – they won't even give it a second look.

When your project is complete and up for sale, consider the pricing of your house slightly lower than the market value because everyone loves a nice new flip house and buyers know the real estate market so well, so when they see a new flip hit the market priced with what looks like a great deal, their feelings will take over and create a sense of urgency. So, don't rely only on realtors to find a property to purchase, I am giving you an option to make research and find deals yourself.

Your ability to flip a house at its reasonably maximum price is also dependent on the current market status, i.e., buyers' or sellers' market.

If the property market's a sellers' market, more people want to buy than those who want to sell. As the law of supply and demand says, when demand is high, and supply is low, prices are high. Because there are fewer properties in the market than buyers, the latter will try to outbid each other for a limited supply of properties, which will drive up property prices. In other words, the best market to flip a house is a sellers' market.

When the market is a buyers' market, the opposite is true. There are more sellers than buyers of properties, and as such, sellers will try to outdo one another by offering the lowest price for their properties just to sell them. When this happens, it will be tough to flip your house at a high price.

Hence, the worst time to flip properties is during a buyers' market. If your investment strategy is buying and holding it for a long time for capital appreciation, a buyers' market is an excellent time to buy.

How Fast Should a Flip Be Completed?

As mentioned earlier, the sooner you're able to finish repairs and renovations, and flip the property, the better. This is because you'll continue to incur maintenance or holding costs by merely holding on to a property.

Another bad sides when it comes to house flipping is that the longer the hold the more money it would costs you in interest payments for the loan. So, the quicker you get it done, the more money you make.

More than just actual holding or maintenance costs, you'll also suffer from possible opportunity losses, especially if there's a significant development in the area that can result in potential price drops for properties in the area. Opportunity losses may also come in the form of missed opportunities to buy another property to flip at a good deal because your capital is still tied to your latest flip, which you haven't completed yet. Remember, the faster you're able to sell the house, the better it'll be for you.

Of Appraisals and Selling Price

Buyers use appraisals to determine reasonable purchase prices for buying properties. But how do appraisers come up with appraisal values for properties?

They do so use sold "comps" – or comparable sales of similar properties – in coming up with appraised values. The challenge with performing appraisals on properties during bullish or appreciating markets is finding enough sold comps for supporting rising appraisal values. This means appraised property values in rising markets tend to be lower than current market values because appraised values are based on past sold comps. This can result in appraisal issues later on.

What kinds of issues? In particular, lower appraised values than what properties similar to yours are currently worth in the market can prevent you from maximizing your selling price. How?

If you already found a buyer for the house you want to flip and that buyer will need to finance the purchase through a mortgage, the appraised value of your property will be the basis for determining the loan amount the buyer can get from his or her financing company. If you're selling or contract price, which is already ok with your buyer, is higher than the appraised value, your buyer's maximum loanable amount for purchasing your house will be lower.

This may keep you from proceeding with the deal, or at best, you'll likely need to drop your price so the buyer can afford to buy the house

CHAPTER 19: Price Home Correctly

through financing at a lower price based on appraised value. You see, most homebuyers – especially those who need bank financing – don't have a lot of extra cash lying around, and if they get a much lower loan to purchase your property, they may not be able to afford it anymore.

This gives you only two options – both of which will prevent you from selling at your desired price. One is to lower the cost just so the deal will push through. The other is to cancel the agreement and look for a new buyer.

However, looking for a new buyer will be challenging, as well. It's because FHA appraisals stick around for four months, which means succeeding buyers within four months from the date of the appraisal will also use that appraisal to secure financing to buy your property. You can only get an updated – and hopefully higher – appraised value that's closer or higher than your desired contract price after four months from the date of the FHA appraisal.

What does this mean, then? Before you spend on repairs and renovation on the property you plan to flip, make sure that their costs won't exceed a level that will keep you from earning your desired ROI if you sell it at its appraised ARV. That way, you minimize the risk of appraisals stopping you from earning your desired ROI.

Chapter 20
Selling Your Home – Negotiation Tips

A negotiation can be defined as a discussion that happens between two or more parties that resolves an issue in a way that each party finds acceptable. Selling your home is one of the biggest financial transactions you will ever engage in your life and the price that is agreed on between you and the buyer, along with the real estate commissions you pay, will determine how much money you walk away with. These negotiating strategies will put you in the driver's seat and help you get top dollar in any market.

KEY STRATEGIES:

1. **Hardball tactic:** this means sticking to your list price or rejecting the offer with no counteroffer.
2. **Only accept offers after an open house:** this will create a sense of competition between the parties.
3. **Counteroffer**: you can simply put an expiration date on it to force a speedy response.
4. You can **agree to pay closing costs** but increase the purchase price.

CHAPTER 20: Selling Your Home – Negotiation Tips

Counter at Your List Price

As a seller, you would most likely reject a potential buyer's initial bid on your home if it's below your asking price. Usually those interested in buying property expect a back-and-forth negotiation, so when they make an offer the initial one will often be lower than the price you planned - and funnily it might also be lower than what they're actually willing to pay.

When this happy what most sellers do is to counteroffer with a price that's higher, but most likely below their listing price, because they do not want to lose the potential sale. They want to be malleable and are mostly willing to negotiate so they can easily close the deal. This strategy does works to the extent that at least you get to sell the property sold, as thousands of sellers will tell you, but this is not the best way to get a good price.

Instead of dropping your price, counter it by sticking to your listed purchase price. If a person is really interested and they want to buy, they will remain engaged and come back to you with an even higher offer. This is assuming of course, that your price is fair to begin with. Not backing down from your list price says that you know what your property is worth, and you intend to get the money you deserve.

Most buyers will be surprised, and some may upset by your unwillingness to negotiate. There is the risk that buyers will walk away when you use this approach. But it can be so helpful by making you avoid wasting time on buyers who make low offers and won't accept any deal unless they can get a bargain.

Another variation of countering at your list price is to counter just a little below it, yielding by perhaps $1,000. You might decide this approach when you want to be tough, but you also don't want to appear too inflexible and drive away buyers.

Reject the Offer

If you're very bold, you can also try this tactic. It is certainly more extreme than countering at your list price: it is pretty simple all you have do to is reject the buyer's offer and don't counter at all. If you still want to keep them in the game, simply ask them to submit a new offer. Be reassured that if they are really interested and you haven't turned them off, they will.

CHAPTER 20: Selling Your Home – Negotiation Tips

For this strategy you need to ask yourself and be certain that your property is worth what you're asking for. If the buyer resubmits, they'll most likely have to make a higher offer— but they may decide to play hardball back and submit the same or even a lower offer.

When you don't counter, you're not locked into a negotiation with any specific buyer and you can accept a higher offer if one comes along. On the side of buyer, him knowing that someone can make a better offer at any moment, he will definitely be creating pressure to submit a more competitive offer quickly if they really want the property. You should use this technique if the property has only been on the market for a short time and if you have an open house coming up.

Create a Bidding War

A bidding war means a situation in which potential buyers of a property vie for ownership via a series of increasing price bids. How can you use it?

Make open houses an integral part of your process. Once you have the home on the market and making it available to be shown, there should be an open house for a few days later. Make sure you do not entertain any offers until after the open house.

Potential buyers or renters will expect to be in competition and may place higher offers because of this assumption. If you get plenty offers, it will be easy for you to go to the top bidders and ask for their highest and best offers. On the other hand, the open house may not bring as many offers as expected but the party offering it won't have an idea about that, so you'll have a psychological edge going forward with counteroffers, etc.

Put an Expiration Date on Your Counteroffer

A counteroffer is a proposal made as a result of an undesirable offer. A counteroffer revises the initial offer and makes it more desirable for the person making the new offer

If a buyer submits an offer that you would like to reject, you can counter his offer. Be informed that then you are involved in a legally binding negotiation with that party and you would not be able to accept a better offer if it comes along.So, if you are interested in selling your property quickly, consider putting an expiration date on your counteroffer. This strategy will compel the person interested in the property to make a decision so you can either get your money or find another buyer.

Be careful not to make the deadline so short that the buyer is turned off, but you should consider making it shorter than the default timeframe in your real estate contract of your state. For example, If the default expiration is three days, you might shorten it to one or two days.

In addition to closing the deal quickly, there's another reason to push landlords to make a fast decision. While the counteroffer is outstanding, your home will be off the market. Most people looking to buy won't submit an offer when another negotiation is underway. And if the deal falls through, you've added time to the official number of days your

CHAPTER 20: Selling Your Home – Negotiation Tips

home has been on the market. You should know that the more days your home is on the market, the less desirable it appears. This is logical. Furthermore, the more likely you are to have to lower your asking price to get a buyer.

Agree to Pay Closing Costs but Increase the Purchase Price

Closing costs are the expenses, beyond the property cost, that buyers and sellers incur to finalize a real estate transaction.

It seems like it's become standard practice for buyers to ask the seller to pay their closing costs. These costs can amount to about 3% of the purchase price and cover what seem to be a lot of frivolous fees. In most cases, some buyers are often feeling cash-strapped from the down payment, moving expenses, the prospect of redecorating costs — and maybe even from paying the closing costs on the home they sold! Some buyers can't afford to close the deal at all without assistance for closing costs.

While many buyers don't have or don't want to spend extra cash up front to get into the home, they can often afford to borrow a little bit more. If you give them the cash, they want for closing costs, the transaction may be more likely to proceed.

When a buyer submits an offer and asks you to pay the closing costs, counter with your willingness to pay but at an increased purchase price, even if it means going above your list price. Buyers sometimes don't realize that when they ask the seller to pay their closing costs, they're effectively lowering the home's sale price. But as the seller, you'll see the bottom line very clearly.

You can increase your asking price by enough to still get as high as your list price after paying the buyer's closing costs. If your list price is $200,000 and the buyer offers $190,000 with $6,000 toward closing, you would counter with something between $196,000 and $206,000 with $6,000 for closing costs.

A catch is that the price plus closing costs must be supported when the home is appraised; otherwise, you'll have to lower it later to close the deal because the buyer's lender won't approve an overpriced sale.

The key to executing these negotiating strategies successfully is that you have to be offering a superior product. The home needs to show well, be in excellent condition and have something that competing properties do not if you want to have the upper hand in negotiations. If buyers aren't excited about the property you're offering, your hardball tactics won't cause them to up their game. They'll just walk away.

Chapter 21
Mistakes Not to Make when Flipping Houses

Buy a house, make a few fixes, put it back on the market, and make a huge profit. This looks so easy! But at that point, the shows on television are good looking, well-dressed investors making the process look fast and profitable. I would advise you to limit your financial risk and maximize your return potential.

INVESTING IN REAL ESTATE: Flipping Houses

Knowing what a house worth doesn't mean you should pay too much on a home but find out how much the maintenance or fixing will cost before you buy. You can figure an ideal purchase price when you have information about the house. Underestimating the time or money the project will cost is the mistakes most real estate investors make.

Investors shouldn't pay more than 70% of the ARV (after repair value) of a property minus the repairs needed, now the ARV is what a home is worth after it's fully repaired. Let's take a look at an example for full understanding: if a home ARV is $140,000 and it needs $30,000 in repairs then the 70% rule means that an investor should pay not more than $68,000 for the home. $140,000 × 0.70 = $98,000 - $30,000 = $68,000

So, flipping business requires time, money, patience, efforts and skills. It may be harder and more expensive than you ever imagine.

Insufficient funds: make a research of your financing option largely, the mortgage that suits your needs and find a lender that requests for low interest. You can use a mortgage calculator which can help you to compare interest rates of various lender offers.

Paying cash for a property eliminate cost of interest, but even when there are opportunity cost and holding cost to tie up your cash. One of the mistake investors make is not having enough money and also you should fully understand how much would cost you by sticking with your proposed project.

CHAPTER 21: Mistakes Not to Make when Flipping Houses

Not enough knowledge: Picking the right property, at the right place, in the right location, should be your priority which shows that you are successful. Even if you get deals of a lifetime, knowing the right renovation and to which to skip is key, you also need to understand the related tax laws and zoning laws and know when to leave a project before it becomes a money pit.

Lack of skills: carpenters, plumbers and painters sometimes flip houses as a side income to their jobs, in which they have the skills and experience to find to fix a house. These people are Professional builders.

Not having enough time: it can take months to find and buy the right house, you would need to invest time to fix up once you own the house. Renovating and flipping houses is a time-consuming investment. So many people might stick to a day job where the earn the same amount of money in weeks or months with constant earnings that has no risk and a consistent time commitment.

Not enough patience: buying a property you see doesn't need a rush, as a professional you either do the work yourself or rely on network reliable contractors.

Newbies would hire a realtor to help them sell the house, but professionals depend on "for sale by owner" to minimize cost and maximize profits. Professionals understands that the profit margins are slim, also buying and selling takes time.

Some things could go wrong for inexperienced or new house flippers

INVESTING IN REAL ESTATE: Flipping Houses

and they should do their research well to start on the right foot. As experienced flippers, we know that, flipping business is a real business not just a hobby. Do you know that most houses that some people cannot willingly buy to renovate, house flippers buy them, renovate them and improve them to the point where there's buyer demand?

Outline a business plan: so why would make a large estate investment without drafting out one? You should firstly draft out a strategic business plan before hoping in, this plan would help investors understand their risk and reward after the house is flipped and sold.

When flipping a house, time is money. A strategic business plan helps real estate investor to estimate their timeline. If house flipping project takes longer time, the more you will pay in carrying cost like financing, property tax and utilities.

Property insurance: purchasing a property insurance shouldn't be something you should forget. Not buying property insurance before you undertake investing project is a mistake.

You would want to do everything you can to protect what you've put into the project if flipping home is all about getting a return on your initial investment.

Choosing the wrong partner: it can make a flip become a flop because investors look for help to anywhere, they can find it. Instead of putting yourself through a stress why not work with a trusted source who are familiar with renovation process and capable to take the project on.

CHAPTER 21: Mistakes Not to Make when Flipping Houses

Always find a realtor you trust, consult with experts who has successfully flipped houses with solid networks among contractors that has great reputation in your area.

Avoid project risk: under improving a property can make a flip business flop. So, when you lose a sale due to under-improving a property it can be a real effort, now, it's better for you to be aware of upcoming industry trends.

Doing the agent work yourself: making research and finding homes to flip for yourself can cause a flop in this business, so no matter how practical or effective you are, there are things you can't fix yourself, I am sure you might be thinking of saving enough money, but why would you prefer saving enough money and ending up losing the money and the business which could become a flop for you.

You can hire professionals and get a house flipped successfully without burning through your cash. You might have decided on doing it yourself but let someone go through the renovation plan with you. The thing is the fact that you're doing it yourself doesn't mean you're saving money. Avoid spending more money because of the mistakes of doing it yourself as a learner.

I'm sure you wouldn't wang to invest in a money pit. Houses with problems are costly to fix, you might end up spending and spending, going through stress and wasting efforts. Investors would help you to see a better home that won't cost you much. It takes months for flipping houses and if you're not well prepared you might lose your sleep over, more reasons why you need to plan properly and ensure you win the game.

Design a house you're flipping according to your taste: you are not flipping this house for yourself. You shouldn't design a house to your taste as someone else should live in it, it's a total waste of money, the person might have a higher taste while yours is lower and vice versa. After flipping the house successfully, the owner of the house might redesign the place and you end of wasting money on designing a house you're not living in. You should avoid a flip that would end up looking like your dream home.

Spending too much on repairs: it is a common pitfall for both new and experienced flippers. Avoid it.

Flippers that takes too much project are causing a risk for themselves. Putting in more than $85,000 - $100,000 into a rehab, this may lead to bigger margins but may has a lot of project risks.

Increase coverage to protect your investment: a strong real estate network will help you succeed in real flipping business, choose the right network with real estate professionals, agents and property sellers, buyers and real estate investors. If I were you, I would put efforts to expanding my own network and stay focus.

Chapter 22

Why Others Fail in Real Estate

Like any business endeavor, there are countless little mistakes new, and even seasoned players can make that will cost them money. A complete failure in this industry can usually be traced back to an investor buying into one of the great real estate fallacies. Even if you're not yet involved and have only done some casual googling of house flipping and residential rental strategies, I'm sure you've seen these dangerous myths perpetuated by all the so-called real estate "gurus" out there: *"House flipping or property rentals are a low-risk source of passive income that only takes good old-fashioned American bravery, grit, and determination to make millions."*

I've seen too many ultra-motivated new investors believe the hype from all the reality TV shows and endless "X tips to make millions flipping houses" articles on the internet, or listen to all those radios shows where some "genius" is laying out their "system"… which usually involves a membership fee of some sort. These normally level-headed investors then dive straight into this business with their minds full of dreams and vague, generic advice, only to crash and burn when the real-world headwinds strike, usually torching their retirement and life savings in the process. And all that carnage could have been avoided if they went into this business clear-eyed and without any fantasies clouding their judgment.

If you're reading this book, then you've already taken a giant leap to ensure that no matter what happens, you won't wind up broken and ruined like thousands of other wannabe investors. The real difference between happy, successful professionals and bitter, bankrupt amateurs has nothing to do with innate skill or luck; it's all about whether they sought out and applied the hard-earned advice of the bloodied investors

CHAPTER 22: Why Others Fail in Real Estate

before them.

This book is designed not to motivate you, but rather arm you with the knowledge and mindset of a savvy real estate investor. To turn amateurs into shrewd professionals who know how to take the guesswork out of investing and manage all forms of risk, all while finding value and creating new equity in the process.

Real estate investing is not some "gentleman's game." Especially nowadays, with so many cash-rich flippers fighting over an ever-shrinking pool of distressed properties. This world is a jungle on the best of days, and an outright battlefield most of the time. Your mental preparation will take far more work than just reading a few pages in a book, but the first step is to rid your mind of all myths and all the hype around flipping homes for a living:

1. Real estate is the exact opposite of "passive income."

Whether you focus on quick flips or long-term renting, you will work your butt off for every dollar you earn. This may be an old industry, but your business is a startup. And have you ever heard a successful entrepreneur brag about how little they work?

When renting, your involvement never ends. Even with a reliable property management company to handle the mundane details, you're still ultimately the landlord, with all the liabilities that entails. So, delegate oversight at your own risk. When flipping, no matter how great a team you assembled, you still must know what to pay for an

INVESTING IN REAL ESTATE: Flipping Houses

investment and find ways to create value by resolving legal and physical issues cheaply while coordinating renovations, agents, lawyers, etc.

At best, if you are not intimately involved in every stage of the operation, you're exposing yourself to new risks. At worst, you're setting yourself up to get ripped off. Remember, before you can collect a payday, there are so many hands reaching into your pockets, such as lawyers, taxmen, contractors, etc. So, if you aren't carefully fact-checking, documenting, and managing everything that's going on, you'll find yourself pulling out nothing but lint from your pockets when the day's over.

If you're employing a pro-investment advisor, make sure to hire them before making a bid on your first house. To get your money's worth out of their service, you want their advice on avoiding making mistakes in the first place, not how to clean up the mess. It might seem like a small note, but agents and advisors should be employed as preventive medicine and not as troubleshooters after you've run into a problem.

Naturally, a great agent can relieve much of this micro-management pressure, but you still can't delegate everything. Plus, the truly reliable professional agents with a long list of references don't come cheap.

2. Real estate requires far more than just cash on hand and a "go-getter" attitude.

Let's face the cold hard reality: you aren't going to discover great investment candidates by cruising the Multiple Listing Service (MLS)

CHAPTER 22: Why Others Fail in Real Estate

or the For Sale by Owner listings on Zillow. The market is too efficient for any lucrative "arbitrage" opportunities to stay available to the general public. So, if you find a great deal that seems too good to be true, odds are it is, and you're missing some nasty surprise. Usually, in the form of some hard to find a lien on the property or structural/site issue that a typical home inspection wouldn't discover.

Even if there is a large mismatch between the asking price and market value, without any hidden problems, the big players, including Zillow itself in some hot markets, will scoop these deals up faster than you can. Even if you're quick, you'll find yourself in a nasty bidding war against competitors with ample cash reserves. Sure, maybe you can get lucky, happens occasionally, but hoping to get lucky is not an investing strategy—that's what gamblers do.

If you're dreaming of simply searching the internet for cheap houses in expensive neighborhoods and expecting to hit the jackpot, you're better off staying out of the real estate game altogether. Just take your cash and head off to a casino. You'll have more fun that way… and probably lose less money.

However, if you're serious about building a real estate empire and minimizing risk while maximizing reward, you need focus. Especially if you follow all the data mining steps, I'll outline shortly; you'll be overwhelmed by all the opportunities and will spread yourself too thin in a hurry. Like with any business, you must focus your efforts on some niche to build a competitive advantage. Now this niche is much easier to create than it sounds. It doesn't mean being the best at everything but finding one thing you can either do better than average or at least what you're most interested in or then pour your energy into dominating that field.

The first thing you have to do is figure out your "niche," or edge. There are countless niches you could carve out. Still, they all revolve around maintaining some type of data advantage; in other words, having some unique information or insight into a slice of the market that isn't common knowledge. The key right now is to realize how incredibly competitive this industry is. If you don't have an edge, you don't have a business plan. And if you're planning on luck, you're planning to fail.

3. Real estate is the very definition of a high-risk investment.

With the margins so tight and so many potential issues that could pop up, many of which are out of your control, there is precious little room for error in this business. It's crucial for investors to fully grasp the risks involved at a visceral level and understand why ruthless risk management is what separates the pros from the bankrupt.

The greatest risks come from:

- Overestimating the amount of equity in a position.
- Overestimating the property's value.
- Failing to estimate your total costs over time realistically.
- Over-renovating properties.

While often overlooked by real estate investing guides, the hands-down

CHAPTER 22: Why Others Fail in Real Estate

biggest risk is not knowing how much equity is in a property before you even purchase. If you know that and only stick to properties with generous cushions of equity, then even if you make a mistake somewhere else, you'll still come out of every deal with a profit. That right, there is the secret to my success.

Maybe the home's value will appreciate later, maybe not. It doesn't matter either way because we aren't in the business of speculating on prices. If that's what excites you, then you should put your money into the stock market. As a professional real estate investor, your business is to hunt down hidden equity before a property gets to market and create new value through smart renovations and clearing debt cheaply. We don't place bets on the future and hope for the best. We buy properties that can generate instant profit now and bet that we can create more profit later, but even if we're wrong, there's a generous cushion of existing wealth to limit our risk.

Professional flippers will never place a bid unless there's already a comfortable equity spread at the current market value. Even then, they want to see extra opportunities to add even more value before prioritizing this project above any others. So, if you're wrong about any aspect of the equity evaluation process, then you're dead in the water from the get-go. Anything else you do later can only limit your losses, but likely won't ever return a profit.

With that said, knowing the current equity and potential equity you can add isn't a matter of guesswork. It's a straightforward list of due diligence items to check, with only a small potential margin of error. You've probably heard all the caveats from different "gurus" saying you'll never be completely sure what a property is worth... but that just shows how little they truly understand the details of flipping residential properties. I've sold 95% of my 300+ flips in the last nine years at exactly the price I originally estimated I could move them for. This has nothing to do with luck, nor do I have some magic "system" or secret formula.

It's all a numbers game, and I just do my homework. Granted, my niche is structuring deals in unique ways to unlock maximum value from the property's debt load, but that wouldn't even be possible without careful analysis to find out how much value is hidden in the current price. You can replicate this same success by following the straightforward principles I lay out in this guide.

This is why it's important to rein in your enthusiasm in the planning stages and ensure you leave plenty of wiggle room in every phase of the process. Especially make sure you limit your financial leverage, include a realistic margin of error in your valuation, sell pricing and renovation estimates, and above all, create a flexible exit strategy to guarantee you can pull out with a profit even if everything turns against you, in short, realistic risk management.

Chapter 23

How to Face Future Risks

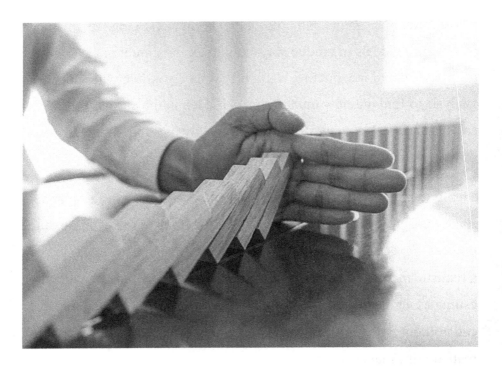

1. Facing Risks Head-On

There is a wide range of risks involved when flipping houses. However, if you are prepared for those risks, you can face them head-on. Being made is the best way to handle unfortunate situations. It is also essential to keep your end goal in mind. Even if things don't go exactly as planned, making money is your end goal, so preserving your potential profits is essential.

2. Planning for Major Expenses or Renovations

Major expenses and renovations don't have to be a major risk when flipping a house if you are aware of them and plan for them correctly. If you can conduct a full interior and exterior inspection of the house before buying it, you will be aware of any major problems. You can figure that into your renovation costs and potential profit. If you were unable to inspect both the inside and the outside, you might not be fully prepared.

3. Unexpected Repairs

Not all renovations and repairs need to be major. In some cases, it is a series of small repairs that cause you to go over budget. When flipping a house, there are a million little details that individually don't seem important, but when trying to market a house to prospective buyers, these details will matter.

Once again, the best way to plan for unexpected repairs is to have as few as possible. The more you know about the house before you buy it, the more prepared you will be going into the project. However, you will handle unexpected repairs the same way you will handle everything:

CHAPTER 23: How to Face Future Risks

with the end goal.

Identifying the Source of the Problem: The first thing you want to do when dealing with an unexpected repair is to identify the source of the problem. This can mean a number of things. First, the repair could be an indication of a larger problem. For example, a crumbling ceiling can be a sign of water damage. Identifying the larger problem is essential to mitigating costs. Fixing the smaller problem will lead to more problems in the future because the larger problem was ignored.

Another thing to consider is if someone is at fault for the unexpected repair. For example, say you bring in a painting contractor to paint the interior of the house, and one of their workers cracks the ceiling by pushing too hard with a stippling brush. The needed repair is the responsibility of the painting contractor. While you might want to be a "nice guy" about it and say, "no big deal," the repair will eat into your potential profits. This goes the same for all contractors you bring in to work on the project.

4. Making Repair Decisions

When repair decisions need to be made, you need to keep your end goal in mind. You are in this to make money, so the first thing you need to ask yourself is if repairing is essential and will help you make money on the flip. For example, you may personally like to replace the kitchen counter. However, if the kitchen counter is in good condition and not notably outdated, there isn't a reason to replace it. This can go the same for larger repairs. If there is a shed on the property that needs a lot of work to make it usable or safe, it may be more cost-effective to tear it down and sell it without a shed than to repair the shed.

5. Unforeseen Expenses

Unforeseen expenses can be more than just repairs. Any unplanned expense needs to be carefully thought out to protect your potential profit. It is also important to stay calm and face each unforeseen expense head-on. Simply reacting to a bad situation or making an emotional decision will be costly and likely unproductive. You want first to examine the situation and the expense and then handle the expense.

How to Handle Unexpected Expenses: The first thing you need to do is remain calm. Evaluate the expense and why it occurred. See if you can mitigate the expense by simply speaking with the powers that be. In some situations, if you just explain yourself, you can reduce or eliminate fines and fees. If you are unable to reduce or eliminate the extra expense, you may be able to set up a payment plan or work out a future deal. Going back to the dumpster example, if you need the dumpster for a couple of extra days, you can contact a representative from the dumpster company and work to develop a relationship. Explain the need for the dumpster and the prospect of future contracts if they are willing to work with you.

6. Contractor Fails and Mistakes

Even if you've worked with a contractor multiple times, contractors fail, and mistakes can happen, and they can cost you valuable time and

CHAPTER 23: How to Face Future Risks

money. The first thing you need to do is establish relationships with contractors you can trust and enjoy working with. Having a relationship with the contractors will minimize the risk of failure and mistakes, but it will also put more pressure on the contractors to fix their mistakes. Any successful contractor will want to maintain a positive relationship to secure future work.

7. Vandalism and Theft

While the house is being renovated, building materials and tools will be in the house. This can make it a target for theft. The house will also be empty, which can make it a target for vandalism. Often, when there is theft, it is of the tools or equipment the thieves can carry out. These items can be easily resold or pawned, which makes them desirable to thieves. Vandalism can be a completely separate issue. Vandalism is often the work of teenagers and may include them hanging out inside the house.

How to Handle Vandalism and Theft: If you encounter theft or vandalism, it is important to get the police involved, so the incident is properly documented. It is also important to get an accurate list of the damage and the value of the things stolen for your insurance company. If you go to the house and suspect someone is inside the house, it is best not to investigate yourself. Be safe, stay in your vehicle, and call the police.

Ways to Prevent Vandalism and Theft: One way to avoid these

INVESTING IN REAL ESTATE: Flipping Houses

problems is to ask the neighbors to keep an eye on the house for you when you aren't there. Give them your number and let them know they can call you if they see a problem. Another thing you can do is secure the house as quickly as possible. It may be difficult first to start working on the house to secure it due to doors and windows being repaired or replaced. However, securing the house will deter or at least slow down some vandals and thieves.

You should also avoid leaving things outside the house. If something valuable is found outside the house, the person who found it might be more motivated to try to get into the house, so all tools and materials should be secured inside the house at the end of each day. Finally, you can buy some relatively inexpensive security cameras for the property. These can allow you to monitor the property remotely, and if there is a problem, catching it on the camera will increase the likelihood that the perpetrators will get caught.

While there are several more potential risks, it is important to be ready and willing to face those risks head-on. There is always a solution; you just have to stay calm and think clearly. Other possible risks include the discovery of liens on the property, issues with neighbors, and issues with the utilities going into the house. There are a wide variety of potential problems that could arise from these situations.

8. Liens

Liens are debts attached to the property. When buying a house in foreclosure, it is the buyer's responsibility to perform their due diligence in investigating liens against the property. A lien can also be a nonmonetary interest in the property. Without careful research, you could inherit debts attached to the property. Liens can be researched through the clerk of courts where the property is located. There are five basic types of liens you should be aware of: easements, judgments, mortgages, real property taxes, and unpaid federal and state income taxes.

9. Neighbor Issues

There are a variety of potential problems you may encounter with the neighbors. Whenever dealing with neighbors, it is important to keep in mind that these are not going to be your neighbors. You need to keep emotions out of it if you have an unpleasant encounter with the neighbors. Some of the issues you encounter may include a property line dispute, complaints about the noise or mess made during renovations, or even arguments rooted in a disagreement the neighbor had with the previous owner.

However, you want the neighbors to support your efforts to renovate the house. If the neighbors feel you are fixing up the neighborhood and helping to increase their property value, they will likely be helpful. This can come in handy, particularly if you encounter theft or vandalism problems. Since you won't be living in the house, the house may become a target for thieves looking to get tools or building materials that they can quickly scrap, pawn, or resell. Neighbors can help to keep an eye on

INVESTING IN REAL ESTATE: Flipping Houses

the problem when you are not there.

10. City or Utility Issues

Sometimes you find issues with the utilities coming into the house that you will need to resolve with the utility companies. When these problems arise, it is important to contact the utility company as quickly as possible. In many situations, if the problem is not life-threatening, you are at the mercy of the utility company's schedule. In some cases, it may take days or even weeks to get the problem resolved. You don't want this to hold renovations or the sale of the property.

11. When Your House Does Not Sell Quickly

Another risk you will take regardless of how many houses you flip will be the risk of not selling the house quickly. The key to really making money is to turn over the houses quickly. However, that requires being able to sell the house as soon as the renovations are finished. Now, if the house is fully renovated, it is priced well, and selling shouldn't be a problem in a growing neighborhood. The risk is that you never know what can change after you buy the house. If the property doesn't sell, you won't make any money on the deal, and you will lose the money you invested in the project. Not selling is probably the greatest risk people worry about when considering house flipping.

Another option is to keep the house as a rental property. You won't immediately get your investment back, but you will have money every month over time. The landlord industry's pros and cons are extensive

CHAPTER 23: How to Face Future Risks

and consuming, so you want to look into the possibility before making a decision entirely. While landlords may look like "easy money" to some, there is a great deal of work involved in owning rentals, and they come with their extensive list of risks, financial and otherwise.

Conclusion

Here we are at the final overview of all the excellent information you have just been fed. If you feel like you have been drinking from a fire hose, go back and reread parts that seem overwhelming or want to digest. Use this book as a systematic approach to engaging in real estate investing for cash flow a reality for you.

This book has been written for you and the hopes that you can take the information in here and internalize it and make it work for you in your

Conclusion

geographic area so that you can become the successful real estate investor you knew you could be.

If we look at the book as a whole, use this as a tool that you will be able to use to set yourself up on the right road.

We have looked at ways to set up your business entity and ways to make sure that what you are setting up reflects what you want to do. We shared many ways to market yourself so that you can start generating lists of leads to buy investment properties and listings of people to sell them too. We looked at many different ways to make cash flow and learned that no one way is the same for each investor. Opening up the thought that every real estate investor encounters challenges, but with the right outlook and a calm approach, you can find a way through the trials and meet the needs of all parties involved. Finally, we realized that the potential to quit your job could be a reality with the right planning and efforts.

While real estate investing is not rocket science, it can require just as much thought and planning. Ensuring that all the pieces of the puzzle are in place to visualize the whole image of success is easy when you have a blueprint or a path to follow already forged by other investors.

Fear is a liar. It comes in to steal your confidence and tries to overshadow the knowledge you have to complete a deal and make consistent cash flow. When fear arrives at your mind's door, you can do one of 2 things 1) Face Everything and Run or 2) Face Everything and

Rise. Choose to rise and face fear. Challenge yourself to step outside of your comfort zone and shake off the negativity you hold on to or that others throw on you that you cannot succeed in this industry in unconventional ways. Engage in as much self-preparation information you can get and implement the nuggets that resonate with you. Be kind to those who doubted you, and when you succeed, do not boast and say, "I told you so!" instead offer to bring them into the circle of success and bless them with the same opportunity you have been successful at.

You have to know in your deep "WHY" soul that you have done right by yourself treat others well and with respect, and that when you lay your head on your pillow at night, you gave a 100% effort to take the next step to reach your goals. We know that in times of trouble, you will take steps backward - come back to this book and regroup. Begin again. The great thing about investing in real estate is that there is always another deal to be done, so remembering that a failed deal today means you are closer to complete the transaction tomorrow.

Thank you for making it through to the end of this book.

We are confident in saying that we know from personal experience real estate investing can change your life, and we hope you found the book informative, and we were able to provide you with all of the tools you need to achieve your goals whatever they may be.

Enjoy the life in real estate investing, and we hope to see you in some of the investment circles in your area someday.

CPSIA information can be obtained
at www.ICGtesting.com
Printed in the USA
LVHW080418130121
676319LV00006B/63